THE LOW CHOLESTEROL COOKBOOK: E   ... FLAVORFUL
DISHES FOR A HAPPY HEART

First edition. March 18, 2024.

Copyright © 2024 Gupta Amit.

ISBN: 979-8223702726

Written by Gupta Amit.

Table of Contents

Quinoa and roasted vegetable salad...1

Chicken and vegetable kebabs 3

Grilled tofu with chimichurri sauce 5

Garlicky roasted broccoli with quinoa......................................7

Stir-fried tofu with snow peas...9

Grilled vegetable platter 11

Baked cod with lemon dill sauce 13

Chickpea and spinach salad..15

Vegetable and lentil curry...17

Stuffed zucchini boats with ground turkey............................19

Caprese skewers with balsamic glaze 21

Lentil and quinoa salad 23

Grilled swordfish with pineapple salsa...................................25

Roasted vegetable and feta frittata 27

Cucumber and red onion salad...29

Baked falafel with cucumber yogurt sauce 31

Grilled halibut with mango salsa..33

Ratatouille with whole wheat pasta..35

Spinach and ricotta stuffed chicken breast.............................37

Black bean and corn quinoa salad 39

Roasted red pepper and lentil soup..41

Asparagus and feta omelette..43

Grilled eggplant with balsamic glaze......................................45

Lentil and vegetable wraps..47

Roasted vegetable and hummus bowls....................................49

Chicken and vegetable stir-fry 51

Stuffed bell peppers with quinoa..53

Spaghetti squash with marinara and turkey meatballs............55

Lentil and barley stew...57

Quinoa and roasted vegetable bowls 59

Grilled tofu with peanut sauce 61

Garlicky roasted Brussels sprouts with quinoa.......................63

Stir-fried tofu with broccoli and carrots.................................65

Grilled vegetable platter with hummus...67
Baked cod with lemon and herb seasoning.......................................69
Chickpea and kale salad...71
Turkey and white bean chili..73
Stuffed acorn squash with quinoa pilaf...75
Caprese salad skewers with balsamic drizzle.....................................77
Lentil and quinoa tabbouleh salad..79
Grilled swordfish with peach salsa..81
Roasted vegetable and goat cheese omelette.....................................83
Tofu and broccoli stir-fry..85
Cucumber and cherry tomato salad..87
Baked falafel with lemon tahini dressing..89
Grilled halibut with tropical fruit salsa...91
Grilled chicken breast with roasted vegetables.................................93
Baked salmon with lemon and herbs...95
Quinoa salad with fresh vegetables...97
Lentil soup with spinach..99
Baked cod with cherry tomatoes...101
Chickpea and vegetable curry...103
Grilled shrimp skewers with pineapple..105
Turkey meatballs with whole wheat pasta...107
Brown rice and black bean bowl..109
Baked halibut with asparagus...111
Hummus and vegetable wrap...113
Baked sweet potato with black beans...115
Lemon garlic shrimp with quinoa...117
Vegetable and bean soup...119
Egg white omelette with spinach and tomatoes..............................121
Baked chicken tenders with whole wheat breadcrumbs.................123
Spinach and mushroom quiche..125
Baked tilapia with mango salsa..127
Cucumber and tomato salad...129
Roasted cauliflower with Parmesan cheese.......................................131

The Low Cholesterol Cookbook: Easy And Flavorful Dishes For A Happy Heart

Quinoa and roasted vegetable salad

Ingredients:

- 1 cup quinoa
- 1 red bell pepper, diced
- 1 zucchini, diced
- 1 yellow squash, diced
- 1/4 cup olive oil
- 2 tbsp balsamic vinegar
- Salt and pepper to taste

Equipment:

1. Chef's knife
2. Cutting board
3. Mixing bowl
4. Baking sheet
5. Oven mitts
6. Salad spinner

Methods:

Step 1: Preheat the oven to 400°F.

Step 2: Wash and chop your favorite vegetables such as bell peppers, zucchini, and cherry tomatoes.

Step 3: Toss the vegetables in olive oil, salt, pepper, and any desired herbs or spices.

Step 4: Spread the vegetables in a single layer on a baking sheet and roast for 20-25 minutes, or until tender and slightly caramelized.

Step 5: While the vegetables are roasting, cook the quinoa according to package instructions.

Step 6: Allow the quinoa and vegetables to cool slightly before combining in a large bowl.

Step 7: Add in any additional ingredients such as feta cheese, nuts, or a vinaigrette dressing.

Step 8: Serve warm or cold and enjoy your delicious quinoa and roasted vegetable salad!

Helpful Tips:

1. Rinse quinoa before cooking to remove any bitterness.

2. Use a ratio of 1:2 quinoa to water for cooking.

3. Add a pinch of salt to the water when cooking quinoa for added flavor.

4. Roast vegetables at a high temperature (around 425°F) for a crispy texture.

5. Drizzle vegetables with olive oil and season with herbs and spices before roasting.

6. Add a variety of colorful vegetables for a visually appealing salad.

7. Mix cooked quinoa with roasted vegetables and toss with a light vinaigrette dressing.

8. Top with fresh herbs or nuts for added crunch and flavor.

9. Chill salad in the refrigerator before serving for a refreshing dish.

Chicken and vegetable kebabs

Ingredients:

- 1 lb boneless, skinless chicken breast
- 1 red bell pepper
- 1 yellow bell pepper
- 1 red onion
- 1 zucchini
- 2 tbsp olive oil
- 2 cloves garlic
- Salt and pepper to taste

Equipment:

1. Skewers
2. Grill pan
3. Tongs
4. Cutting board
5. Knife
6. Mixing bowl

Methods:

Step 1: Soak wooden skewers in water for at least 30 minutes.

Step 2: Cut boneless, skinless chicken breasts into 1-inch cubes.

Step 3: Cut red bell peppers, zucchini, and red onions into similar-sized pieces.

Step 4: Marinate chicken and vegetables in a mixture of olive oil, garlic, lemon juice, and your favorite spices.

Step 5: Thread chicken and vegetables onto skewers, alternating between the ingredients.

Step 6: Preheat grill to medium-high heat and oil the grates to prevent sticking.

Step 7: Grill kebabs for 10-12 minutes, turning occasionally, until chicken is cooked through and vegetables are tender.

Step 8: Serve hot and enjoy!

Helpful Tips:

1. Marinate the chicken and veggies in a flavorful blend of olive oil, lemon juice, garlic, and herbs for at least 30 minutes.

2. Use metal skewers or soak wooden skewers in water for at least 30 minutes to prevent them from burning.

3. Alternate pieces of chicken and vegetables on the skewers for even cooking.

4. Preheat your grill or broiler to high heat before cooking the kebabs.

5. Cook the kebabs for 10-15 minutes, turning them occasionally to ensure they cook evenly.

6. Serve the kebabs with a side of rice or a salad for a complete meal.

Grilled tofu with chimichurri sauce

Ingredients:
- 1 block of tofu
- 2 tbsp olive oil
- 2 garlic cloves
- 1/4 cup fresh parsley
- 1/4 cup red wine vinegar
- 1/2 tsp red pepper flakes
- Salt and pepper to taste

Equipment:
1. Grill
2. Tongs
3. Brush
4. Mixing bowl
5. Cutting board
6. Knife

Methods:
Step 1: Press tofu to remove excess water.

Step 2: Cut tofu into desired shape and size.

Step 3: Preheat grill to medium-high heat.

Step 4: Brush tofu with oil and season with salt and pepper.

Step 5: Place tofu on the grill and cook for 4-5 minutes on each side, until grill marks form.

Step 6: In the meantime, prepare chimichurri sauce by blending parsley, cilantro, garlic, red pepper flakes, vinegar, and olive oil in a food processor.

Step 7: Once tofu is cooked, serve with chimichurri sauce on top.

Step 8: Enjoy your delicious Grilled tofu with chimichurri sauce!

Helpful Tips:
1. Press the tofu beforehand to remove excess water and improve the texture before grilling.

2. Marinate the tofu in a mixture of olive oil, garlic, parsley, and red wine vinegar before grilling for added flavor.

3. Make sure your grill is hot before adding the tofu to achieve those desired grill marks.

4. Prepare the chimichurri sauce in advance and let it sit for a few hours to allow the flavors to meld together.

5. Serve the grilled tofu with a generous drizzle of chimichurri sauce on top for a delicious and vibrant dish.

Garlicky roasted broccoli with quinoa

Ingredients:
- 1 head of broccoli
- 2 cloves of garlic
- 1 cup of quinoa
- Olive oil, salt, pepper to taste

Equipment:
1. Baking sheet
2. Mixing bowl
3. Whisk
4. Saucepan
5. Cooking spoon

Methods:
Step 1: Preheat the oven to 400°F (200°C).

Step 2: Wash and cut one head of broccoli into florets.

Step 3: In a bowl, toss the broccoli florets with olive oil, minced garlic, salt, and pepper.

Step 4: Spread the seasoned broccoli on a baking sheet in a single layer.

Step 5: Roast in the oven for 20-25 minutes, or until the broccoli is tender and slightly browned.

Step 6: While the broccoli is roasting, cook quinoa according to package instructions.

Step 7: Serve the garlicky roasted broccoli over a bed of cooked quinoa.

Step 8: Enjoy your delicious and healthy meal!

Helpful Tips:
1. Start by preheating your oven to 425°F.

2. Toss broccoli florets with olive oil, minced garlic, salt, and pepper in a bowl.

3. Spread the seasoned broccoli on a baking sheet in a single layer.

4. Roast in the oven for 20-25 minutes, or until the broccoli is tender and slightly crispy.

5. Meanwhile, cook quinoa according to package instructions.

6. Once both the broccoli and quinoa are done, mix them together in a large bowl.

7. Taste and adjust seasoning as needed, adding more salt or pepper if desired.

8. Serve hot as a delicious and healthy meal.   .

Stir-fried tofu with snow peas

Ingredients:

- 1 block of tofu
- 2 cups snow peas
- 3 cloves garlic
- 1 tsp soy sauce
- 1 tsp sesame oil
- Salt and pepper

Equipment:

1. Wok
2. Spatula
3. Cutting board
4. Knife
5. Mixing bowl

Methods:

Step 1: Press tofu to remove excess water and cut into small cubes.

Step 2: Heat oil in a wok or skillet over medium-high heat.

Step 3: Add tofu cubes and cook until browned on all sides.

Step 4: Remove tofu from the pan and set aside.

Step 5: Add snow peas to the pan and stir-fry until they are bright green and tender.

Step 6: Return tofu to the pan and stir to combine with the snow peas.

Step 7: Add soy sauce, garlic, ginger, and any other desired seasonings.

Step 8: Cook for another 1-2 minutes, then serve hot.

Helpful Tips:

1. Make sure to press the tofu beforehand to remove excess moisture and improve texture.

2. Cut the tofu into small cubes to ensure even cooking and better absorption of flavors.

3. Heat up the wok or skillet before adding the oil to prevent sticking.

4. Use high heat and continuously stir the tofu to achieve a nice sear and crispiness.

5. Add the snow peas towards the end of cooking to maintain their crunchiness.

6. Season with soy sauce, garlic, ginger, and a touch of sesame oil for an authentic Asian flavor.

7. Garnish with sesame seeds or chopped green onions for added freshness.

Grilled vegetable platter

Ingredients:
- 1 red bell pepper
- 1 yellow bell pepper
- 1 zucchini
- 1 eggplant
- 1/4 cup olive oil
- Salt and pepper to taste
- 2 tablespoons balsamic vinegar

Equipment:
1. Knife
2. Cutting board
3. Grill pan
4. Tongs
5. Vegetable peeler

Methods:
Step 1: Preheat the grill to medium-high heat.

Step 2: Cut your favorite vegetables into bite-sized pieces (such as bell peppers, zucchini, eggplant, and cherry tomatoes).

Step 3: Toss the vegetables in olive oil, salt, pepper, and any desired seasonings or herbs.

Step 4: Place the vegetables on the preheated grill, turning occasionally to ensure even cooking.

Step 5: Grill the vegetables until they are charred and tender, about 8-10 minutes.

Step 6: Arrange the grilled vegetables on a serving platter.

Step 7: Drizzle with balsamic glaze or a vinaigrette dressing before serving.

Step 8: Enjoy your delicious grilled vegetable platter!

Helpful Tips:
1. Choose a variety of colorful vegetables such as bell peppers, zucchini, mushrooms, and cherry tomatoes for a visually appealing presentation.

2. Cut vegetables into similar sizes to ensure even cooking on the grill.

3. Marinate vegetables in a mixture of olive oil, garlic, herbs, and balsamic vinegar for added flavor.

4. Use a grilling basket or skewers to prevent vegetables from falling through the grill grates.

5. Preheat the grill before adding the vegetables to ensure they cook evenly.

6. Rotate vegetables occasionally to prevent burning and ensure all sides are cooked.

7. Garnish the platter with fresh herbs or a squeeze of lemon juice before serving.

Baked cod with lemon dill sauce

Ingredients:
- 4 cod fillets
- 1 lemon
- 1/4 cup dill
- 1/2 cup Greek yogurt
- Salt and pepper
- Olive oil

Equipment:
1. Baking dish
2. Mixing bowl
3. Whisk
4. Fish spatula
5. Saucepan
6. Lemon squeezer

Methods:
Step 1: Preheat your oven to 400°F.

Step 2: Season the cod fillets with salt and pepper.

Step 3: Place the cod fillets in a baking dish.

Step 4: In a small bowl, mix together melted butter, lemon juice, dill, and garlic.

Step 5: Pour the lemon dill sauce over the cod fillets.

Step 6: Cover the baking dish with foil.

Step 7: Bake the cod in the preheated oven for 15-20 minutes, or until the fish is opaque and flakes easily with a fork.

Step 8: Serve the baked cod with the lemon dill sauce drizzled on top. Enjoy!

Helpful Tips:
1. Preheat your oven to 400°F.
2. Season your cod fillets with salt, pepper, and a squeeze of lemon juice.
3. Place the fillets in a baking dish and drizzle with olive oil.

4. Bake for 15-20 minutes, or until the fish is opaque and flakes easily with a fork.

5. While the fish is baking, make the lemon dill sauce by mixing together mayonnaise, lemon juice, chopped dill, and a pinch of salt.

6. Serve the baked cod with the lemon dill sauce drizzled on top.

7. Garnish with additional dill and lemon slices for an extra pop of flavor. Enjoy!

Chickpea and spinach salad

Ingredients:

- 1 can of chickpeas
- 4 cups of fresh spinach
- 1 red onion
- 1 lemon

Equipment:

1. Mixing bowl
2. Skillet
3. Tongs
4. Knife
5. Cutting board

Methods:

Step 1: Start by rinsing and draining a can of chickpeas.

Step 2: In a large mixing bowl, combine the chickpeas with chopped fresh spinach.

Step 3: Add diced red onion, cherry tomatoes, and cucumber to the bowl.

Step 4: In a separate small bowl, whisk together olive oil, lemon juice, minced garlic, salt, and pepper to create the dressing.

Step 5: Pour the dressing over the salad ingredients and toss to coat everything evenly.

Step 6: Let the salad sit in the refrigerator for at least 30 minutes to allow the flavors to meld together.

Step 7: Serve and enjoy your delicious chickpea and spinach salad.

Helpful Tips:

1. Rinse and drain a can of chickpeas to remove excess sodium.

2. Mix together olive oil, lemon juice, salt, and pepper as the dressing.

3. Gently sauté the spinach with garlic for added flavor.

4. Add chopped red onion and cherry tomatoes for a pop of color and freshness.

5. For extra protein, toss in grilled chicken or tofu.

6. Sprinkle feta cheese or toasted nuts on top for a crunchy texture.

7. Feel free to customize with your favorite herbs and spices like cumin or paprika.

8. Serve chilled or at room temperature for a refreshing side dish.

Vegetable and lentil curry

Ingredients:
- 1 cup red lentils
- 1 onion, chopped
- 2 cloves garlic, minced
- 1 tbsp curry powder
- 1 can coconut milk
- 2 cups mixed veggies
- 1 cup vegetable broth

Equipment:
1. Knife
2. Cutting board
3. Saucepan
4. Wooden spoon
5. Ladle

Methods:
Step 1: Heat oil in a large pot and add chopped onions, garlic, and ginger.

Step 2: Cook until onions are soft, then add curry powder and cumin.

Step 3: Stir in chopped vegetables such as carrots, bell peppers, and zucchini.

Step 4: Add red lentils and vegetable broth to the pot.

Step 5: Bring to a boil, then reduce heat and simmer for 20-25 minutes, stirring occasionally.

Step 6: Add coconut milk and let simmer for another 5 minutes.

Step 7: Season with salt and pepper to taste.

Step 8: Serve hot with rice or naan bread. Enjoy your vegetable and lentil curry!

Helpful Tips:
1. Start by heating oil in a large pot and sautéing onions, garlic, and ginger until fragrant.

2. Add your choice of vegetables such as sweet potatoes, carrots, bell peppers, and cauliflower, and cook until slightly tender.

3. Stir in green or red lentils, vegetable broth, canned tomatoes, and curry powder for flavor.

4. Simmer the curry until the lentils are cooked through and the vegetables are tender.

5. For added creaminess, stir in a can of coconut milk towards the end of cooking.

6. Season with salt, pepper, and additional curry powder to taste.

7. Serve over cooked rice or naan bread for a complete meal.

Stuffed zucchini boats with ground turkey

Ingredients:
- 4 medium zucchinis
- 1 lb ground turkey
- 1 cup cooked quinoa
- 1/2 cup shredded cheese

Equipment:
1. Knife
2. Cutting board
3. Mixing bowl
4. Baking dish
5. Skillet

Methods:
Step 1: Preheat the oven to 375°F.

Step 2: Cut zucchinis in half lengthwise and scoop out the seeds to create boats.

Step 3: In a skillet, cook ground turkey until browned.

Step 4: Add minced garlic, diced onions, and bell peppers to the skillet. Cook until soft.

Step 5: Season with salt, pepper, and your favorite spices.

Step 6: Mix in cooked quinoa or rice to the turkey mixture.

Step 7: Fill the zucchini boats with the turkey mixture.

Step 8: Top with shredded cheese and breadcrumbs.

Step 9: Bake for 25-30 minutes until the zucchinis are tender. Enjoy your delicious stuffed zucchini boats!

Helpful Tips:
1. Start by preheating your oven to 375°F.

2. Halve the zucchinis lengthwise and scoop out the seeds to create boats.

3. In a skillet, cook ground turkey with onions, garlic, and your favorite seasonings until browned.

4. Fill the zucchini boats with the cooked turkey mixture.

5. Top with shredded cheese and breadcrumbs for added flavor and texture.

6. Bake in the oven for about 20-25 minutes, or until the zucchinis are tender.

7. Garnish with fresh herbs like parsley or basil before serving.

8. Enjoy your delicious and healthy stuffed zucchini boats!

Caprese skewers with balsamic glaze

Ingredients:
- 1 pint cherry tomatoes (16)
- 1 bunch fresh basil leaves
- 8 oz fresh mozzarella balls (16)
- 2 tbsp balsamic glaze

Equipment:
1. Skewers
2. Cutting board
3. Knife
4. Small saucepan
5. Brush

Methods:
Step 1: Begin by slicing cherry tomatoes and fresh mozzarella into bite-sized pieces.

Step 2: Take wooden skewers and thread a piece of tomato, mozzarella, and fresh basil onto each skewer.

Step 3: Arrange the skewers on a serving platter or plate.

Step 4: In a small saucepan, heat balsamic vinegar over medium heat until it thickens and reduces by half to create the glaze.

Step 5: Drizzle the balsamic glaze over the assembled skewers.

Step 6: Season with salt and pepper to taste.

Step 7: Serve and enjoy these delicious Caprese skewers with balsamic glaze!

Helpful Tips:
1. Use fresh, ripe cherry tomatoes and mozzarella cheese for the best flavor.

2. Alternate cherry tomatoes, basil leaves, and mozzarella balls on skewers for a visually appealing presentation.

3. Drizzle a balsamic glaze over the skewers for a sweet and tangy finish.

4. Season with salt and pepper to enhance the flavors of the ingredients.

5. Let the skewers marinate in the balsamic glaze for at least 30 minutes before serving to allow the flavors to meld together.

6. Serve the Caprese skewers as a light and refreshing appetizer or side dish. Enjoy!

Lentil and quinoa salad

Ingredients:

- 1 cup quinoa
- 1 cup lentils
- 1 red bell pepper
- 1 cucumber
- 1/4 cup feta cheese
- 2 tbsp olive oil
- 1 lemon
- Salt and pepper

Equipment:

1. Mixing bowl
2. Cutting board
3. Knife
4. Saucepan
5. Wooden spoon

Methods:

Step 1: Rinse 1 cup of quinoa under cold water and cook according to package instructions.

Step 2: In a separate pot, combine 1 cup of lentils with 2 cups of water and bring to a boil.

Step 3: Reduce heat and simmer for 15-20 minutes until lentils are tender.

Step 4: Drain any excess water from the lentils and let cool.

Step 5: In a large mixing bowl, combine the cooked quinoa and lentils.

Step 6: Add in chopped vegetables such as cucumber, bell peppers, and cherry tomatoes.

Step 7: Drizzle with olive oil and lemon juice, then season with salt and pepper to taste.

Step 8: Toss to combine and serve chilled. Enjoy your delicious Lentil and Quinoa Salad!

Helpful Tips:

1. Rinse quinoa thoroughly before cooking to remove bitterness.

2. Cook quinoa in vegetable or chicken broth for added flavor.

3. Use a 2:1 ratio of liquid to quinoa when cooking.

4. Cook lentils separately from quinoa to prevent mushiness.

5. Season the salad with a dressing of olive oil, lemon juice, and herbs.

6. Add roasted vegetables like bell peppers, zucchini, or cherry tomatoes for extra flavor.

7. Top with feta cheese or toasted nuts for a creamy or crunchy texture.

8. Store salad in an airtight container in the fridge for up to 3 days for easy meal prep.

Grilled swordfish with pineapple salsa

Ingredients:

- 4 swordfish fillets
- 1 small pineapple, diced
- 1 red bell pepper, diced
- 1/4 red onion, diced
- 1/4 cup cilantro, chopped
- 2 tbsp lime juice
- Salt and pepper to taste

Equipment:

1. Grill
2. Knife
3. Cutting board
4. Tongs
5. Mixing bowl

Methods:

Step 1: Preheat the grill to medium-high heat.

Step 2: Season the swordfish steaks with salt, pepper, and olive oil.

Step 3: Place the swordfish steaks on the grill and cook for 4-5 minutes per side, or until the fish is opaque and flakes easily with a fork.

Step 4: While the swordfish is cooking, prepare the pineapple salsa by combining diced pineapple, red onion, jalapeno, cilantro, lime juice, and salt in a bowl.

Step 5: Remove the swordfish from the grill and top with the pineapple salsa.

Step 6: Serve hot and enjoy your delicious grilled swordfish with pineapple salsa.

Helpful Tips:

1. Start by marinating the swordfish in olive oil, lemon juice, garlic, and herbs for at least 30 minutes.

2. Preheat the grill to medium-high heat and oil the grates to prevent sticking.

3. Grill the swordfish for 4-5 minutes per side, or until the fish is opaque and flakes easily with a fork.

4. While the swordfish is grilling, prepare the pineapple salsa by combining diced pineapple, red onion, jalapeno, cilantro, and lime juice in a bowl.

5. Serve the grilled swordfish topped with the pineapple salsa for a fresh and delicious meal.

Roasted vegetable and feta frittata

Ingredients:
- 8 eggs
- 1 red bell pepper
- 1 yellow bell pepper
- 1 zucchini
- 1 red onion
- 100g feta cheese
- 2 tbsp olive oil

Equipment:
1. Frying pan
2. Whisk
3. Spatula
4. Mixing bowl
5. Cutting board
6. Knife

Methods:
Step 1: Preheat the oven to 375°F.

Step 2: Cut up your favorite vegetables into bite-sized pieces (such as bell peppers, zucchini, and cherry tomatoes).

Step 3: In a cast-iron skillet, sauté the vegetables in olive oil until they are slightly softened.

Step 4: In a bowl, whisk together 8 eggs, salt, pepper, and crumbled feta cheese.

Step 5: Pour the egg mixture over the vegetables in the skillet.

Step 6: Transfer the skillet to the oven and bake for 20-25 minutes or until the frittata is set and golden brown.

Step 7: Let it cool slightly before slicing and serving. Enjoy!

Helpful Tips:
1. Preheat your oven to 400°F before you start preparing your ingredients.
2. Cut your vegetables into small, bite-sized pieces for even cooking.

3. Toss your vegetables in olive oil, salt, and pepper before roasting to enhance their flavor.

4. Use a non-stick skillet or cast iron pan for easier clean-up.

5. Beat your eggs with a splash of milk or cream for a fluffy frittata.

6. Layer your roasted vegetables and crumbled feta evenly in the skillet before pouring in the egg mixture.

7. Bake your frittata for about 15-20 minutes or until the center is set and the top is golden brown.

8. Let it cool slightly before slicing and serving. Enjoy!

Cucumber and red onion salad

Ingredients:

- 2 cucumbers
- 1 red onion
- 2 tbsp olive oil
- 1 tbsp red wine vinegar
- Salt and pepper to taste

Equipment:

1. Mixing bowl
2. Whisk
3. Knife
4. Cutting board
5. Salad spinner

Methods:

Step 1: Begin by thinly slicing 1 cucumber and 1 red onion.

Step 2: Place the sliced cucumber and red onion in a large mixing bowl.

Step 3: Add 1/4 cup of white vinegar and 1/4 cup of olive oil to the bowl.

Step 4: Season the salad with salt, pepper, and a pinch of sugar to taste.

Step 5: Toss the salad well to evenly coat the vegetables with the dressing.

Step 6: Cover the bowl and let the salad marinate in the refrigerator for at least 30 minutes.

Step 7: Serve the cucumber and red onion salad chilled as a refreshing side dish. Enjoy!

Helpful Tips:

1. Start by thinly slicing the cucumber and red onion.

2. Soak the sliced red onion in cold water for 10-15 minutes to mellow out the sharp flavor.

3. Use a mandolin to achieve consistently thin cucumber slices.

4. Mix equal parts white vinegar and water to create a simple dressing for the salad.

5. Add a pinch of sugar to balance out the acidity of the vinegar.

6. Fresh herbs like dill or parsley can add a pop of flavor to the salad.

7. Let the salad marinate in the dressing for at least 30 minutes before serving for the best flavor.

8. Season with salt and pepper to taste before serving.

Baked falafel with cucumber yogurt sauce

Ingredients:
- 1 can (15.5 oz) chickpeas
- 1/4 cup chopped onion
- 2 cloves garlic
- 1 tsp cumin
- 1/2 cup plain yogurt
- 1/4 cup diced cucumber
- 1 tbsp lemon juice
- Salt and pepper to taste

Equipment:
1. Baking sheet
2. Food processor
3. Mixing bowl
4. Skillet
5. Spatula

Methods:
Step 1: Preheat the oven to 375°F and line a baking sheet with parchment paper.

Step 2: In a food processor, pulse together 1 can of drained chickpeas, 1/4 cup chopped onion, 2 cloves of minced garlic, 1/4 cup of fresh parsley, 1 tsp of ground cumin, 1/2 tsp of ground coriander, 1/4 tsp of cayenne pepper, 1/4 tsp of salt, and 2 tbsp of olive oil until smooth.

Step 3: Form the mixture into small patties and place them on the prepared baking sheet.

Step 4: Bake for 25-30 minutes or until golden brown.

Step 5: In a separate bowl, mix together 1/2 cup of Greek yogurt, 1/2 cup of diced cucumber, 1 clove of minced garlic, 1 tbsp of lemon juice, and a pinch of salt.

Step 6: Serve the baked falafel with the cucumber yogurt sauce on top. Enjoy!

Helpful Tips:

1. Preheat your oven to 375°F and line a baking sheet with parchment paper.

2. In a food processor, combine chickpeas, onion, parsley, garlic, cumin, coriander, and salt until mixture is well combined but slightly chunky.

3. Form mixture into small patties and place on the baking sheet.

4. Bake falafel for 25-30 minutes, flipping halfway through cooking time, until golden brown and crispy.

5. While falafel is baking, make cucumber yogurt sauce by combining yogurt, chopped cucumber, lemon juice, dill, and salt in a bowl.

6. Serve falafel hot with cucumber yogurt sauce drizzled on top. Enjoy!

Grilled halibut with mango salsa

Ingredients:

- 4 halibut fillets
- 1 mango, diced
- 1 red bell pepper, diced
- 1/4 cup red onion, finely chopped
- 1/4 cup fresh cilantro, chopped
- 1 lime, juiced
- Salt and pepper to taste

Equipment:

1. Grill pan
2. Tongs
3. Chef's knife
4. Cutting board
5. Mixing bowl

Methods:

Step 1: Preheat your grill to medium-high heat.

Step 2: Season halibut fillets with salt, pepper, and a drizzle of olive oil.

Step 3: Place the halibut fillets on the grill and cook for 4-5 minutes per side, or until the fish is opaque and flakes easily with a fork.

Step 4: In a bowl, combine diced mango, red onion, jalapeno, cilantro, lime juice, and salt to make the mango salsa.

Step 5: Serve the grilled halibut topped with the mango salsa.

Step 6: Enjoy your delicious grilled halibut with mango salsa!

Helpful Tips:

1. Start by marinating the halibut in a mixture of olive oil, lemon juice, garlic, and herbs for at least 30 minutes.

2. Preheat your grill to medium-high heat and oil the grates to prevent sticking.

3. Grill the halibut for about 4-5 minutes per side, or until it flakes easily with a fork.

4. While the halibut is cooking, prepare the mango salsa by combining diced mango, red onion, cilantro, jalapeno, and lime juice.

5. Serve the grilled halibut topped with the mango salsa for a fresh and flavorful meal. Enjoy!

Ratatouille with whole wheat pasta

Ingredients:

- 1 onion, diced
- 2 cloves garlic, minced
- 1 zucchini, sliced
- 1 eggplant, diced
- 1 red bell pepper, diced
- 1 cup tomato sauce
- 1 tsp dried herbs
- 8 oz whole wheat pasta

Equipment:

1. Pot
2. Pan
3. Wooden spoon
4. Knife
5. Colander

Methods:

Step 1: Prepare your ingredients - eggplant, zucchini, bell peppers, tomatoes, onion, garlic, whole wheat pasta, olive oil, and herbs.

Step 2: Preheat the oven to 400°F and chop the vegetables into small pieces.

Step 3: Toss the vegetables in olive oil, garlic, and herbs, then spread them out on a baking sheet.

Step 4: Roast the vegetables for 30 minutes, or until they are tender and slightly browned.

Step 5: While the vegetables are roasting, cook the whole wheat pasta according to package instructions.

Step 6: Once the pasta is cooked, toss it with the roasted vegetables and serve hot. Enjoy your delicious ratatouille with whole wheat pasta!

Helpful Tips:

1. Start by chopping all your vegetables (zucchini, eggplant, bell peppers, tomatoes) into small, bite-sized pieces.

2. Sautee the vegetables in olive oil until they are soft and slightly caramelized.

3. Season the vegetables with salt, pepper, and herbs like thyme and basil for added flavor.

4. Cook whole wheat pasta according to package instructions until al dente.

5. Combine the cooked pasta with the ratatouille and gently toss to mix everything together.

6. Feel free to add some grated Parmesan cheese on top for extra richness.

7. Serve hot and enjoy your delicious and nutritious ratatouille with whole wheat pasta.

Spinach and ricotta stuffed chicken breast

Ingredients:
- 4 boneless skinless chicken breasts
- 1 cup ricotta cheese
- 1 cup chopped spinach
- 1/4 cup grated Parmesan cheese
- Salt and pepper to taste

Equipment:
1. Skillet
2. Mixing bowl
3. Knife
4. Tongs
5. Baking dish

Methods:
Step 1: Preheat the oven to 375°F.

Step 2: In a bowl, mix together 1 cup of ricotta cheese, 1 cup of chopped spinach, 1/4 cup of grated Parmesan cheese, and a pinch of salt and pepper.

Step 3: Cut a slit in each chicken breast to create a pocket.

Step 4: Stuff each chicken breast with the spinach and ricotta mixture.

Step 5: Season the chicken breasts with salt, pepper, and any desired herbs or spices.

Step 6: Place the stuffed chicken breasts on a baking sheet.

Step 7: Bake in the preheated oven for 25-30 minutes or until the chicken is cooked through.

Step 8: Serve and enjoy!

Helpful Tips:
1. Begin by pounding the chicken breasts to an even thickness for even cooking.

2. Mix together fresh spinach, ricotta cheese, garlic, and seasonings for the stuffing.

3. Carefully slice a pocket into each chicken breast for the stuffing, being careful not to cut all the way through.

4. Stuff each chicken breast with the spinach and ricotta mixture, being sure not to overfill.

5. Secure the opening of the chicken breast with toothpicks to keep the stuffing in place while cooking.

6. Season the outside of the chicken breasts with salt, pepper, and any additional herbs or spices.

7. Bake in a preheated oven until the chicken is cooked through and the stuffing is hot and bubbly.

8. Let the chicken rest for a few minutes before serving to allow the juices to redistribute. Enjoy!

Black bean and corn quinoa salad

Ingredients:

- 1 cup quinoa
- 1 can black beans
- 1 cup corn
- 1 red bell pepper
- 1/4 cup cilantro
- 1/4 cup lime juice
- 2 tbsp olive oil

Equipment:

1. Mixing bowl
2. Wooden spoon
3. Chef's knife
4. Cutting board
5. Saucepan

Methods:

Step 1: Rinse 1 cup of quinoa under cold water.

Step 2: In a medium saucepan, bring 2 cups of water to a boil.

Step 3: Add the quinoa to the boiling water, cover, and reduce heat to low. Cook for 15-20 minutes.

Step 4: In a large mixing bowl, combine 1 can of black beans (rinsed and drained), 1 cup of corn (frozen or fresh), and 1 diced red bell pepper.

Step 5: In a small bowl, whisk together 1/4 cup of olive oil, 2 tablespoons of lime juice, 1 teaspoon of cumin, and salt to taste.

Step 6: Once the quinoa is cooked, fluff with a fork and let cool.

Step 7: Add the quinoa to the mixing bowl with the black beans, corn, and bell pepper.

Step 8: Pour the dressing over the quinoa mixture and toss to combine.

Step 9: Serve the black bean and corn quinoa salad chilled or at room temperature. Enjoy!

Helpful Tips:

1. Start by rinsing the quinoa thoroughly to remove any bitter coating.

2. Cook the quinoa according to package instructions, using a 1:2 ratio of quinoa to water.

3. In a separate pot, cook the black beans until tender or use canned beans for convenience.

4. Sautee the corn in a skillet with a little olive oil until lightly charred for added flavor.

5. Combine the cooked quinoa, black beans, corn, diced bell peppers, red onions, and cilantro in a large bowl.

6. Dress the salad with a lime vinaigrette made with lime juice, olive oil, garlic, cumin, and salt.

7. Toss the salad gently to evenly distribute the flavors.

8. Serve chilled or at room temperature for a refreshing and nutritious meal.

Roasted red pepper and lentil soup

Ingredients:

- 2 red peppers
- 1 cup red lentils
- 1 onion
- 3 cloves garlic
- 4 cups vegetable broth
- Salt and pepper
- Olive oil

Equipment:

1. Large soup pot
2. Blender
3. Cutting board
4. Knife
5. Wooden spoon

Methods:

Step 1: Preheat your oven to 400 degrees Fahrenheit.

Step 2: Place 2 red bell peppers on a baking sheet and roast in the oven for 20-25 minutes, until the skins are charred.

Step 3: Remove the peppers from the oven and let them cool. Peel off the charred skin, remove the seeds, and chop the peppers into small pieces.

Step 4: In a large pot, heat olive oil over medium heat and sauté 1 onion and 2 cloves of garlic until softened.

Step 5: Add 1 cup of dried red lentils, chopped roasted red peppers, 4 cups of vegetable broth, and 1 teaspoon of cumin to the pot.

Step 6: Bring the soup to a boil, then reduce heat and let simmer for 20-25 minutes, until the lentils are cooked through.

Step 7: Use an immersion blender to blend the soup until smooth. Season with salt and pepper to taste.

Step 8: Serve the soup hot, garnished with a dollop of Greek yogurt and fresh parsley. Enjoy!

Helpful Tips:

1. Begin by roasting the red peppers to enhance their flavor.

2. Use a high-quality vegetable or chicken broth as the base of the soup.

3. Cook the lentils separately and add them to the soup towards the end of the cooking process.

4. Blend the soup until smooth for a creamy texture.

5. Season with salt, pepper, and any other desired herbs or spices.

6. Serve the soup hot with a drizzle of olive oil or a dollop of Greek yogurt on top.

7. Garnish with chopped fresh herbs or a sprinkle of Parmesan cheese for added flavor.

Asparagus and feta omelette

Ingredients:
- 8 large eggs
- 1 bunch of asparagus
- 1/2 cup crumbled feta
- Salt and pepper
- 2 tbsp olive oil

Equipment:
1. Frying pan
2. Whisk
3. Spatula
4. Mixing bowl
5. Chef's knife

Methods:
Step 1: Heat a non-stick skillet over medium heat.

Step 2: In a bowl, whisk together 2 eggs with salt and pepper.

Step 3: Add 1/4 cup of chopped asparagus to the egg mixture.

Step 4: Pour the egg mixture into the skillet and cook for 2-3 minutes.

Step 5: Sprinkle 1/4 cup of crumbled feta cheese over half of the omelette.

Step 6: Fold the omelette in half and cook for an additional 1-2 minutes.

Step 7: Slide the omelette onto a plate and serve hot.

Step 8: Enjoy your delicious asparagus and feta omelette!

Helpful Tips:
1. Start by whisking eggs and seasoning with salt and pepper.

2. Heat a non-stick skillet over medium heat and add a drizzle of olive oil.

3. Add chopped asparagus and cook until slightly tender, about 2-3 minutes.

4. Pour in the beaten eggs and swirl to evenly distribute the asparagus.

5. Cook until the edges start to set, then crumble feta cheese over the top.

6. Use a spatula to fold the omelette in half and continue cooking until the cheese melts.

7. Slide the omelette onto a plate and garnish with fresh herbs or a sprinkle of red pepper flakes.

8. Serve hot and enjoy your delicious asparagus and feta omelette!

Grilled eggplant with balsamic glaze

Ingredients:
- 1 large eggplant
- 2 tbsp olive oil
- 2 tbsp balsamic vinegar
- Salt and pepper to taste

Equipment:
1. Grill pan
2. Tongs
3. Basting brush
4. Knife
5. Cutting board

Methods:
Step 1: Preheat the grill to medium-high heat.

Step 2: Cut the eggplant into 1/2 inch thick slices.

Step 3: Brush the eggplant slices with olive oil on both sides.

Step 4: Place the eggplant slices on the grill and cook for 5-7 minutes per side, or until tender and grill marks form.

Step 5: In a small saucepan, bring balsamic vinegar to a simmer and cook until it has reduced by half.

Step 6: Drizzle the balsamic glaze over the grilled eggplant slices.

Step 7: Serve the grilled eggplant with balsamic glaze as a side dish or appetizer. Enjoy!

Helpful Tips:
1. Preheat your grill to medium-high heat.

2. Slice the eggplant into 1/2 inch rounds.

3. Brush the eggplant slices with olive oil and sprinkle with salt and pepper.

4. Grill the eggplant slices for 3-4 minutes per side, or until they are tender and have grill marks.

5. In a small saucepan, heat balsamic vinegar and honey over low heat until it thickens, about 5-7 minutes.

6. Drizzle the balsamic glaze over the grilled eggplant before serving.

7. Garnish with fresh herbs or Parmesan cheese for added flavor.

8. Enjoy your delicious grilled eggplant with balsamic glaze!

Lentil and vegetable wraps

Ingredients:

- 1 cup cooked lentils
- 1/2 red bell pepper, diced
- 1/2 cucumber, sliced
- 1 carrot, shredded
- 4 whole grain wraps

Equipment:

1. Skillet
2. Knife
3. Cutting board
4. Mixing bowl
5. Tongs

Methods:

Step 1: Cook 1 cup of lentils in boiling water for 20 minutes until tender.

Step 2: Sauté 1 diced onion, 2 minced garlic cloves, and 1 diced bell pepper in olive oil.

Step 3: Add 1 diced zucchini, 1 diced carrot, and 1 diced tomato to the pan and cook until vegetables are soft.

Step 4: Season with salt, pepper, cumin, and chili powder to taste.

Step 5: Warm up wraps in a skillet.

Step 6: Fill each wrap with a scoop of lentils and vegetable mixture.

Step 7: Garnish with fresh cilantro and a squeeze of lime juice.

Step 8: Roll up the wraps and enjoy!

Helpful Tips:

1. Start by cooking the lentils according to package instructions, usually simmering in water for about 20-30 minutes until tender.

2. While the lentils are cooking, prep your favorite vegetables such as bell peppers, cucumbers, tomatoes, and lettuce for the wraps.

3. Consider adding some additional protein such as tofu, chickpeas, or grilled chicken for a heartier option.

4. To assemble the wraps, lay out a tortilla and fill with a scoop of cooked lentils, veggies, and protein if desired.

5. Drizzle with your favorite sauce or dressing, such as tahini, hummus, or a vinaigrette for added flavor.

6. Roll up the wrap tightly and enjoy a healthy and delicious meal.

Roasted vegetable and hummus bowls

Ingredients:
- 2 bell peppers (sliced)
- 2 zucchinis (sliced)
- 1 red onion (sliced)
- 1 cup cherry tomatoes
- 1 cup hummus
- 4 cups cooked quinoa
- 4 tbsp olive oil
- Salt and pepper to taste
(129 characters)

Equipment:
1. Knife
2. Cutting board
3. Baking sheet
4. Mixing bowl
5. Blender
6. Serving bowl

Methods:
Step 1: Preheat the oven to 400°F.

Step 2: Chop a variety of your favorite vegetables, such as carrots, bell peppers, zucchini, and red onion.

Step 3: Toss the vegetables with olive oil, salt, and pepper on a baking sheet.

Step 4: Roast the vegetables in the oven for 25-30 minutes, or until they are tender and caramelized.

Step 5: While the vegetables are roasting, prepare the hummus by blending chickpeas, tahini, lemon juice, garlic, and olive oil in a food processor until smooth.

Step 6: Divide the roasted vegetables among bowls and top with a generous dollop of hummus.

Step 7: Enjoy your delicious and nutritious roasted vegetable and hummus bowls!

Helpful Tips:

1. Preheat your oven to 400°F to ensure even cooking of the vegetables.

2. Cut the vegetables into uniform sizes to ensure they cook evenly.

3. Toss the vegetables in olive oil, salt, and any desired herbs or seasonings before roasting.

4. Use a large baking sheet lined with parchment paper to roast the vegetables, for easy cleanup and to prevent sticking.

5. Check and stir the vegetables occasionally while roasting to prevent burning or uneven cooking.

6. Allow the roasted vegetables to cool slightly before assembling your bowl to prevent wilting the greens.

7. Top with a generous dollop of hummus and sprinkle with additional seasonings or garnishes before serving.

8. Enjoy your delicious and nutritious roasted vegetable and hummus bowl!

Chicken and vegetable stir-fry

Ingredients:

- 1 lb chicken breast
- 1 red bell pepper
- 1 yellow bell pepper
- 1 cup broccoli florets
- 1/4 cup soy sauce
- 2 tbsp vegetable oil
- 2 cloves garlic
- 1 tsp ginger
- Salt and pepper to taste

Equipment:

1. Wok
2. Wooden spatula
3. Chef's knife
4. Cutting board
5. Tongs

Methods:

Step 1: Heat a tablespoon of oil in a large skillet or wok over medium-high heat.

Step 2: Add diced chicken breast and cook until browned and cooked through.

Step 3: Remove chicken from skillet and set aside.

Step 4: Add more oil to the skillet and stir in sliced vegetables such as bell peppers, broccoli, and carrots.

Step 5: Cook vegetables until slightly tender, but still crisp.

Step 6: Add the chicken back to the skillet and pour in a stir-fry sauce of your choice.

Step 7: Stir everything together and cook for an additional 2-3 minutes.

Step 8: Serve over rice or noodles and enjoy!

Helpful Tips:

1. Start by marinating your chicken in a mixture of soy sauce, ginger, and garlic for at least 30 minutes.

2. Use a high-heat oil like peanut or canola oil for stir-frying to get a nice sear on the chicken.

3. Cook the chicken first until it is no longer pink before adding in your vegetables.

4. Cut your vegetables into uniform sizes to ensure even cooking.

5. Add in your vegetables in order of longest cooking time, such as bell peppers before snow peas.

6. Don't overcook your vegetables, they should still have a slight crunch.

7. Season with additional soy sauce, sesame oil, and red pepper flakes for added flavor.

Stuffed bell peppers with quinoa

Ingredients:
- 4 bell peppers
- 1 cup quinoa
- 1 can black beans
- 1 cup corn kernels
- 1 cup diced tomatoes
- 1 tsp cumin
- Salt and pepper to taste

Equipment:
1. Knife
2. Cutting board
3. Mixing bowl
4. Skillet
5. Spoon
6. Baking dish

Methods:
Step 1: Preheat the oven to 375°F.

Step 2: Cut the tops off of bell peppers and remove the seeds and ribs.

Step 3: In a large bowl, mix cooked quinoa, diced vegetables, diced tomatoes, and seasonings.

Step 4: Spoon the quinoa mixture into the bell peppers until they are full.

Step 5: Top with cheese and cover with the pepper tops, if desired.

Step 6: Place the stuffed peppers in a baking dish and add a little water to the bottom of the dish.

Step 7: Cover the dish with foil and bake for about 30-35 minutes.

Step 8: Remove from the oven, let cool slightly, and enjoy!

Helpful Tips:
1. Preheat your oven to 375°F.
2. Cook quinoa according to package instructions and set aside.
3. Cut the tops off the bell peppers and remove seeds and membranes.

4. In a large skillet, sauté onions, garlic, and any other desired vegetables until tender.

5. Add cooked quinoa, your choice of protein, and seasonings to the skillet and mix well.

6. Stuff the bell peppers with the quinoa mixture, packing it in tightly.

7. Place the stuffed peppers in a baking dish and cover with foil.

8. Bake for 25-30 minutes, then remove foil and bake for an additional 10 minutes.

9. Serve hot and enjoy!

Spaghetti squash with marinara and turkey meatballs

Ingredients:
- 1 large spaghetti squash
- 1 lb ground turkey
- 1 cup marinara sauce
- 1 tsp Italian seasoning

Equipment:
1. Knife
2. Cutting board
3. Pot
4. Wooden spoon
5. Colander
6. Baking sheet

Methods:
Step 1: Preheat oven to 400°F.

Step 2: Cut spaghetti squash in half lengthwise and remove seeds.

Step 3: Place squash halves face down on a baking sheet and bake for 30-40 minutes, or until tender.

Step 4: While squash is baking, prepare turkey meatballs according to package instructions.

Step 5: Heat marinara sauce in a saucepan on the stove.

Step 6: Once squash is cooked, use a fork to scrape out the flesh into long strands.

Step 7: Serve spaghetti squash in bowls, top with marinara sauce and turkey meatballs.

Step 8: Enjoy!

Helpful Tips:
1. Preheat your oven to 400 degrees Fahrenheit.
2. Cut the spaghetti squash in half lengthwise and scoop out the seeds.

3. Place the squash halves face down on a baking sheet and bake for 45-50 minutes, or until tender.

4. While the squash is cooking, prepare your turkey meatballs using ground turkey, breadcrumbs, egg, and seasonings.

5. Bake the meatballs in the oven for 20-25 minutes, or until cooked through.

6. Heat marinara sauce in a separate saucepan on the stove.

7. Once the squash is cooked, use a fork to scrape out the strands into a bowl.

8. Serve the spaghetti squash topped with marinara sauce and turkey meatballs. Enjoy!

Lentil and barley stew

Ingredients:

- 1 cup lentils
- 1/2 cup barley
- 1 onion, diced
- 2 carrots, chopped
- 4 cups vegetable broth
- 1 tsp garlic powder
- 1 tsp cumin
- Salt and pepper to taste

Equipment:

1. Pot
2. Wooden spoon
3. Chef's knife
4. Cutting board
5. Ladle

Methods:

Step 1: Heat olive oil in a large pot over medium heat.

Step 2: Add chopped onions, carrots, and celery to the pot and cook until softened.

Step 3: Stir in minced garlic, cumin, and paprika and cook for a minute.

Step 4: Add vegetable broth, lentils, barley, diced tomatoes, and bay leaves to the pot.

Step 5: Bring the mixture to a boil, then reduce heat to low and simmer for 30 minutes.

Step 6: Season with salt and pepper to taste.

Step 7: Add chopped spinach and cook for an additional 5 minutes.

Step 8: Serve hot and enjoy your lentil and barley stew!

Helpful Tips:

1. Rinse the lentils and barley before cooking to remove any dirt or debris.

2. Use a mix of vegetables like carrots, celery, and onions for added flavor and nutrition.

3. Season with herbs like thyme, bay leaves, and garlic for a tasty and aromatic stew.

4. Consider using vegetable broth instead of water for a richer flavor.

5. Simmer the stew on low heat for at least an hour to allow the flavors to develop.

6. Serve with a dollop of Greek yogurt or a sprinkle of fresh parsley for extra freshness.

7. Enjoy with a side of crusty bread for a satisfying meal.

Quinoa and roasted vegetable bowls

Ingredients:

- 1 cup quinoa
- 1 red bell pepper, sliced
- 1 zucchini, sliced
- 1 small red onion, sliced
- 1 tablespoon olive oil
- 1 teaspoon garlic powder
- 1/2 teaspoon paprika

Equipment:

1. Chef's knife
2. Cutting board
3. Mixing bowl
4. Baking sheet
5. Frying pan

Methods:

Step 1: Preheat the oven to 400°F.

Step 2: Chop your favorite vegetables, such as bell peppers, zucchini, and red onion.

Step 3: Toss the vegetables with olive oil, salt, and pepper on a baking sheet.

Step 4: Roast the vegetables in the oven for 25-30 minutes, or until they are golden brown and tender.

Step 5: While the vegetables are roasting, rinse the quinoa under cold water.

Step 6: Bring 2 cups of water to a boil in a medium saucepan and add the quinoa.

Step 7: Reduce heat to a simmer, cover, and cook for 15 minutes.

Step 8: Fluff the quinoa with a fork and divide it among bowls.

Step 9: Top the quinoa with the roasted vegetables and enjoy!

Helpful Tips:

1. Rinse quinoa thoroughly before cooking to remove any bitterness.

2. Use a 2:1 ratio of water to quinoa for fluffy, perfectly cooked grains.

3. Season the quinoa with salt, pepper, and a squeeze of lemon juice for added flavor.

4. Roast a variety of colorful vegetables at a high temperature to bring out their natural sweetness.

5. Toss the roasted vegetables with olive oil, garlic, and your favorite herbs before serving.

6. Add protein such as grilled chicken, chickpeas, or tofu to make the bowl more filling.

7. Top the bowl with a creamy dressing or sauce for extra richness.

Grilled tofu with peanut sauce

Ingredients:
- 1 block of tofu
- 1/4 cup of soy sauce
- 1/4 cup of peanut butter
- 2 tbsp of rice vinegar
- 2 cloves of garlic
- 1 tsp of ginger
- 1 tbsp of sesame oil

Equipment:
1. Grill pan
2. Tongs
3. Mixing bowl
4. Whisk
5. Saucepan

Methods:
Step 1: Preheat your grill to medium-high heat.

Step 2: Cut a block of firm tofu into slices or cubes.

Step 3: Brush the tofu slices with a bit of oil to prevent sticking.

Step 4: Place the tofu on the grill and cook for about 3-4 minutes on each side, until grill marks appear and tofu is heated through.

Step 5: In the meantime, prepare the peanut sauce by combining peanut butter, soy sauce, lime juice, garlic, and ginger in a bowl.

Step 6: Serve the grilled tofu with the peanut sauce drizzled on top and enjoy!

Helpful Tips:
1. Press the tofu before grilling to remove excess water and improve texture.

2. Marinate the tofu in soy sauce, garlic, and ginger for extra flavor.

3. Preheat your grill to medium-high heat before adding the tofu.

4. Grill the tofu for 5-7 minutes on each side, until it has grill marks and is heated through.

5. Make a peanut sauce by whisking together peanut butter, soy sauce, lime juice, and sriracha.

6. Serve the grilled tofu with the peanut sauce drizzled on top.

7. Garnish with chopped peanuts and fresh cilantro for extra crunch and flavor.

Garlicky roasted Brussels sprouts with quinoa

Ingredients:

- 400g Brussels sprouts
- 1/4 cup olive oil
- 4 cloves of garlic
- 1 cup quinoa
- Salt and pepper
- 1/2 lemon
- Fresh parsley

Equipment:

1. Baking sheet
2. Whisk
3. Saucepan
4. Knife
5. Cutting board

Methods:

Step 1: Preheat the oven to 400°F.

Step 2: Trim and halve Brussels sprouts.

Step 3: Toss Brussels sprouts with olive oil, minced garlic, salt, and pepper.

Step 4: Spread Brussels sprouts on a baking sheet in a single layer.

Step 5: Roast in the oven for 25-30 minutes, or until crispy and browned.

Step 6: While Brussels sprouts are roasting, cook quinoa according to package instructions.

Step 7: Once Brussels sprouts are done, toss them with cooked quinoa.

Step 8: Serve hot and enjoy your garlicky roasted Brussels sprouts with quinoa!

Helpful Tips:

1. Preheat your oven to 400°F (200°C) and line a baking sheet with parchment paper.

2. Wash and trim the Brussels sprouts, then cut them in half.

3. Toss the Brussels sprouts with olive oil, minced garlic, salt, and pepper.

4. Spread the Brussels sprouts evenly on the baking sheet and roast for about 25-30 minutes, until crispy and golden brown.

5. While the Brussels sprouts are roasting, cook quinoa according to package instructions.

6. Once the quinoa is cooked, mix in some chopped fresh herbs like parsley or cilantro for extra flavor.

7. Serve the roasted Brussels sprouts on a bed of quinoa and enjoy!

Stir-fried tofu with broccoli and carrots

Ingredients:
- 1 block of tofu
- 2 cups of broccoli
- 1 cup of carrots
- 2 tbsp of vegetable oil

Equipment:
1. Wok
2. Spatula
3. Chef's knife
4. Cutting board
5. Steamer basket
6. Mixing bowl

Methods:
Step 1: Heat a wok or large skillet over medium-high heat.

Step 2: Add 1 tablespoon of vegetable oil to the wok.

Step 3: Add 1 block of diced tofu to the hot oil and stir-fry until golden brown, about 5-7 minutes.

Step 4: Remove the tofu from the wok and set aside.

Step 5: Add 1 tablespoon of vegetable oil to the wok.

Step 6: Add 1 cup of sliced carrots and 2 cups of broccoli florets to the hot oil and stir-fry for 3-4 minutes.

Step 7: Return the tofu to the wok and toss everything together.

Step 8: Season with soy sauce, garlic, ginger, and red pepper flakes to taste.

Step 9: Stir-fry for an additional 2-3 minutes until heated through.

Step 10: Serve hot over rice or noodles. Enjoy your stir-fried tofu with broccoli and carrots!

Helpful Tips:
1. Press tofu in paper towels to remove excess water before slicing into cubes.

2. Heat oil in a non-stick pan on medium-high heat.

3. Stir-fry tofu until lightly browned on all sides.

4. Remove tofu from pan and set aside.

5. Add more oil to the pan and stir-fry broccoli and carrots until tender-crisp.

6. Add tofu back to the pan and toss with vegetables.

7. Season with soy sauce, garlic, and ginger for flavor.

8. Serve hot over rice or noodles.

9. Garnish with sesame seeds or green onions for extra taste.

10. Enjoy your delicious and healthy stir-fried tofu with broccoli and carrots!

Grilled vegetable platter with hummus

Ingredients:
- 2 zucchinis, sliced
- 2 bell peppers, sliced
- 1 eggplant, sliced
- 1 red onion, sliced
- 1 cup hummus
- Olive oil, salt, and pepper to taste

Equipment:
1. Grill
2. Knife
3. Cutting board
4. Mixing bowl
5. Tongs

Methods:
Step 1: Preheat the grill to medium-high heat.

Step 2: Wash and chop a variety of vegetables such as bell peppers, zucchini, eggplant, and cherry tomatoes.

Step 3: Toss the vegetables with olive oil, salt, and pepper.

Step 4: Grill the vegetables, turning occasionally, until they are charred and tender.

Step 5: In the meantime, prepare the hummus by blending chickpeas, tahini, lemon juice, garlic, and olive oil in a food processor.

Step 6: Once the vegetables are cooked, arrange them on a platter.

Step 7: Serve the grilled vegetables with the hummus on the side for dipping. Enjoy your delicious and healthy meal!

Helpful Tips:
1. Preheat your grill to medium-high heat.

2. Cut a variety of colorful vegetables into uniform sizes for even cooking.

3. Toss the vegetables in olive oil, salt, pepper, and any other desired seasonings.

4. Place the vegetables on the grill and cook until tender, flipping halfway through.

5. Keep a close eye on the veggies to prevent burning.

6. While the vegetables cook, prepare a simple hummus by blending chickpeas, tahini, lemon juice, garlic, and olive oil.

7. Serve the grilled vegetables on a platter with the hummus on the side for dipping.

8. Garnish with fresh herbs or a drizzle of balsamic glaze for added flavor.

Baked cod with lemon and herb seasoning

Ingredients:
- 4 cod fillets
- 1 lemon
- 2 tbsp olive oil
- 1 tsp dried herbs

Equipment:
1. Baking dish
2. Mixing bowl
3. Whisk
4. Cooking brush
5. Knife

Methods:
Step 1: Preheat the oven to 400°F.

Step 2: Place the cod fillets on a baking sheet lined with parchment paper.

Step 3: In a small bowl, mix together lemon juice, olive oil, minced garlic, chopped parsley, salt, and pepper.

Step 4: Brush the lemon and herb mixture over the cod fillets.

Step 5: Bake in the preheated oven for 15-20 minutes, or until the cod is cooked through and flakes easily with a fork.

Step 6: Serve the baked cod garnished with extra lemon slices and chopped parsley. Enjoy your delicious and flavorful meal!

Helpful Tips:
1. Preheat your oven to 400 degrees Fahrenheit.

2. Coat the cod fillets with olive oil and season generously with salt and pepper.

3. Squeeze fresh lemon juice over the cod and sprinkle on your favorite herbs (such as parsley, thyme, or dill).

4. Place the cod on a baking sheet lined with parchment paper.

5. Bake in the preheated oven for 15-20 minutes, or until the fish is cooked through and flakes easily with a fork.

6. Serve the baked cod with additional lemon wedges for squeezing and enjoy with your favorite side dishes.

Chickpea and kale salad

Ingredients:
- 2 cans of chickpeas, drained
- 1 bunch of kale, chopped
- 1/4 cup of olive oil
- 2 tablespoons of lemon juice
- Salt and pepper to taste

Equipment:
1. Knife
2. Cutting board
3. Mixing bowl
4. Salad spinner
5. Tongs

Methods:
Step 1: Rinse and drain one can of chickpeas.

Step 2: Preheat the oven to 400°F.

Step 3: Toss the chickpeas with olive oil, salt, and pepper on a baking sheet.

Step 4: Roast the chickpeas for 20-25 minutes, until crispy.

Step 5: In a large bowl, massage chopped kale with olive oil and lemon juice.

Step 6: Add diced cucumber, cherry tomatoes, and red onion to the kale.

Step 7: Mix in the roasted chickpeas.

Step 8: Drizzle with a simple vinaigrette made of olive oil, lemon juice, Dijon mustard, and honey.

Step 9: Season with salt and pepper to taste.

Step 10: Enjoy your delicious chickpea and kale salad!

Helpful Tips:
1. Start by rinsing and draining a can of chickpeas before roasting them in the oven with olive oil and seasonings for added flavor and crunch.

2. Massage the kale leaves with a bit of olive oil and lemon juice to help soften them and reduce bitterness.

3. Incorporate other colorful and nutritious ingredients like cherry tomatoes, red onion, and feta cheese for extra flavor and texture.

4. Make a simple vinaigrette dressing with olive oil, lemon juice, Dijon mustard, and honey to drizzle over the salad right before serving.

5. Top the salad with toasted nuts or seeds for a satisfying crunch and added protein. Enjoy!

Turkey and white bean chili

Ingredients:

- 1 lb ground turkey
- 1 can white beans
- 1 onion
- 3 cloves garlic
- 1 can diced tomatoes
- 1 can chicken broth
- 1 tsp cumin
- 1 tsp chili powder
- 1/2 tsp red pepper flakes
- Salt and pepper to taste

Equipment:

1. Knife
2. Cutting board
3. Wooden spoon
4. Pot
5. Ladle

Methods:

Step 1: Heat olive oil in a large pot over medium heat.

Step 2: Add chopped onions, garlic, and diced turkey to the pot.

Step 3: Cook until turkey is browned and onions are translucent.

Step 4: Stir in diced tomatoes, chicken broth, cumin, chili powder, and oregano.

Step 5: Bring the mixture to a simmer and let it cook for 20 minutes.

Step 6: Add white beans and corn to the pot and continue cooking for an additional 10 minutes.

Step 7: Season with salt and pepper to taste.

Step 8: Serve hot with toppings like shredded cheese, sour cream, and chopped cilantro. Enjoy your Turkey and white bean chili!

Helpful Tips:

1. Start by browning the ground turkey in a large pot for added flavor.

2. Add in diced onions, bell peppers, and garlic for a flavorful base.

3. Season with chili powder, cumin, and oregano for a classic chili taste.

4. Stir in canned white beans and diced tomatoes for protein and texture.

5. Add chicken broth to create a hearty broth for the chili.

6. Let the chili simmer on low heat for at least 30 minutes to let the flavors meld together.

7. Serve with your favorite toppings like avocado, cilantro, and shredded cheese.

8. Enjoy with cornbread or tortilla chips for a complete meal.

Stuffed acorn squash with quinoa pilaf

Ingredients:
- 2 acorn squash
- 1 cup quinoa
- 1/2 cup dried cranberries
- 1/4 cup chopped pecans
- 1/4 cup crumbled feta
- 1 tsp dried thyme
- Salt and pepper

Equipment:
1. Chef's knife
2. Cutting board
3. Mixing bowl
4. Wooden spoon
5. Baking sheet
6. Saucepan

Methods:
Step 1: Preheat the oven to 375°F.

Step 2: Cut the top off of the acorn squash and scoop out the seeds.

Step 3: Place the squash halves on a baking sheet and brush them with olive oil.

Step 4: Roast the squash in the oven for 30-35 minutes, until fork-tender.

Step 5: While the squash is roasting, prepare the quinoa pilaf according to package instructions.

Step 6: Once the squash is cooked, fill each half with the quinoa pilaf mixture.

Step 7: Return the stuffed squash to the oven and bake for an additional 10-15 minutes.

Step 8: Serve and enjoy your stuffed acorn squash with quinoa pilaf.

Helpful Tips:
1. Start by preheating your oven to 375°F.

2. Cut the acorn squash in half and scoop out the seeds.

3. Brush the squash with olive oil and season with salt and pepper.

4. Place the squash halves face down on a baking sheet and roast for 30 minutes.

5. While the squash is roasting, prepare the quinoa pilaf according to package instructions.

6. Mix in diced vegetables, herbs, and dried fruit to the cooked quinoa.

7. Fill the roasted squash halves with the quinoa pilaf mixture.

8. Return to the oven for an additional 15 minutes.

9. Garnish with fresh herbs before serving. Enjoy!

Caprese salad skewers with balsamic drizzle

Ingredients:
- Cherry tomatoes (16)
- Fresh basil leaves (32)
- Mozzarella balls (16)
- Balsamic glaze (4 tbsp)

Equipment:
1. Skewers
2. Mixing bowl
3. Whisk
4. Cutting board
5. Knife
6. Saucepan

Methods:
Step 1: Begin by gathering cherry tomatoes, fresh basil leaves, and small mozzarella balls.

Step 2: Thread one cherry tomato, one basil leaf, and one mozzarella ball onto a skewer.

Step 3: Repeat step 2 with all the remaining ingredients until all skewers are assembled.

Step 4: Arrange the skewers on a serving platter.

Step 5: Drizzle balsamic glaze over the skewers for added flavor.

Step 6: Serve the Caprese salad skewers immediately as an appetizer or side dish. Enjoy!

Helpful Tips:
1. Use fresh ingredients - opt for ripe cherry tomatoes, fresh basil leaves, and high-quality mozzarella cheese.

2. Alternate cherry tomatoes, basil leaves, and mozzarella cubes on skewers for a beautiful presentation.

3. Drizzle balsamic glaze over the skewers for a sweet tangy flavor.

4. Season with salt and pepper to enhance the flavors.

5. Let the skewers chill in the refrigerator for at least 30 minutes before serving to allow the flavors to meld together.

6. Serve as a light and refreshing appetizer or snack for a summer gathering.

Lentil and quinoa tabbouleh salad

Ingredients:
- 1 cup cooked quinoa
- 1 cup cooked lentils
- 1 cucumber, diced
- 1 tomato, diced
- 1/4 cup chopped fresh parsley
- 1/4 cup chopped fresh mint
- 1/4 cup lemon juice
- 2 tbsp olive oil
- Salt and pepper to taste

Equipment:
1. Mixing bowl
2. Cutting board
3. Knife
4. Pot
5. Spoon

Methods:
Step 1: Rinse 1 cup of quinoa under cold water and cook according to package instructions.

Step 2: In a separate pot, cook 1 cup of lentils in 2 cups of water until tender.

Step 3: Finely chop 1 cucumber, 1 red bell pepper, 1 red onion, and a handful of fresh parsley.

Step 4: In a large bowl, mix the cooked quinoa and lentils with the chopped vegetables.

Step 5: Add 1/4 cup of olive oil, the juice of 1 lemon, and salt and pepper to taste.

Step 6: Mix everything together and let it sit in the fridge for at least 30 minutes before serving. Enjoy your Lentil and quinoa tabbouleh salad!

Helpful Tips:

1. Rinse the quinoa and lentils thoroughly before cooking to remove any bitterness.

2. Cook the quinoa and lentils separately according to package instructions to ensure both are cooked perfectly.

3. Chop all vegetables finely for easy mixing and better texture in the salad.

4. Mix in fresh herbs like parsley, mint, or cilantro for added flavor.

5. Add a squeeze of fresh lemon juice and a drizzle of olive oil for a bright and refreshing dressing.

6. Season with salt, pepper, and any additional spices to taste.

7. Let the salad chill in the refrigerator for at least 30 minutes before serving to allow the flavors to meld.

Grilled swordfish with peach salsa

Ingredients:
- 4 swordfish fillets
- 2 peaches
- 1 red onion
- 1 jalapeno
- 1/4 cup cilantro
- 1 lime
- Salt and pepper

Equipment:
1. Grill pan
2. Tongs
3. Chef's knife
4. Cutting board
5. Mixing bowl
6. Serving platter

Methods:
Step 1: Preheat the grill to medium-high heat.

Step 2: Season swordfish steaks with salt, pepper, and olive oil.

Step 3: Grill swordfish steaks for 4-5 minutes per side, or until cooked through.

Step 4: While swordfish is grilling, prepare the peach salsa by combining diced peaches, red onion, jalapeno, cilantro, lime juice, and salt in a bowl.

Step 5: Remove swordfish from the grill and top with peach salsa.

Step 6: Serve grilled swordfish with peach salsa and enjoy!

Helpful Tips:
1. Start by marinating the swordfish in a mixture of olive oil, garlic, lemon juice, and herbs for at least 30 minutes.

2. Preheat your grill to medium-high heat and brush the grates with oil to prevent sticking.

3. Grill the swordfish for about 4-5 minutes per side, or until it is cooked through and has nice grill marks.

4. While the swordfish is cooking, prepare the peach salsa by mixing diced peaches, red onion, jalapeno, cilantro, and lime juice in a bowl.

5. Serve the grilled swordfish topped with the peach salsa for a fresh and flavorful dish. Enjoy!

Roasted vegetable and goat cheese omelette

Ingredients:
- 8 eggs
- 1/2 cup goat cheese
- 1 red bell pepper
- 1 zucchini
- 1 red onion
- 2 tbsp olive oil
- Salt and pepper to taste

Equipment:
1. Frying pan
2. Whisk
3. Spatula
4. Chef's knife
5. Cutting board

Methods:
Step 1: Preheat the oven to 400°F and prepare a baking sheet with parchment paper.

Step 2: Chop an assortment of your favorite vegetables, such as bell peppers, onions, and zucchini.

Step 3: Toss the vegetables with olive oil, salt, and pepper, then spread them out on the baking sheet.

Step 4: Roast the vegetables in the oven for 20-25 minutes, or until they are tender and slightly caramelized.

Step 5: In a separate bowl, whisk together eggs, salt, and pepper.

Step 6: Pour the egg mixture into a heated skillet and cook until it begins to set.

Step 7: Add the roasted vegetables and crumbled goat cheese to one side of the omelette.

Step 8: Fold the omelette in half and cook for another minute or until the cheese is melted.

Step 9: Serve hot and enjoy your delicious roasted vegetable and goat cheese omelette!

Helpful Tips:

1. Preheat your oven to 400°F before starting to roast the vegetables.

2. Cut the vegetables into evenly sized pieces to ensure even cooking.

3. Toss the vegetables with olive oil, salt, and pepper before roasting to enhance their flavor.

4. Use a non-stick skillet to cook the omelette and prevent it from sticking.

5. Beat the eggs with a splash of milk for a light and fluffy omelette.

6. Cook the eggs over low heat to prevent them from browning too quickly.

7. Once the eggs are nearly set, add the roasted vegetables and goat cheese to one side of the omelette.

8. Fold the omelette in half and let it cook for another minute before serving hot.

Tofu and broccoli stir-fry

Ingredients:

- 1 block of tofu, diced
- 2 cups of broccoli florets
- 2 cloves of garlic, minced
- 1 tablespoon of soy sauce
- 1 tablespoon of sesame oil
- 1 teaspoon of ginger, grated

Equipment:

1. Wok
2. Spatula
3. Tongs
4. Knife
5. Cutting board

Methods:

Step 1: Cut a block of firm tofu into bite-sized cubes and pat dry with paper towels.

Step 2: Heat a tablespoon of oil in a skillet over medium heat.

Step 3: Add the tofu to the skillet and cook until golden brown on all sides.

Step 4: Remove the tofu from the skillet and set aside.

Step 5: In the same skillet, add another tablespoon of oil and stir-fry chopped broccoli until tender-crisp.

Step 6: Add the tofu back to the skillet and season with soy sauce, garlic, and ginger.

Step 7: Cook for an additional 2-3 minutes, then serve hot over rice or noodles.

Helpful Tips:

1. Press the tofu before cooking to remove excess moisture and improve texture.

2. Use a non-stick pan or wok for stir-frying to prevent sticking.

3. Start by stir-frying the tofu until it is golden brown on all sides.

4. Don't overcrowd the pan - cook the tofu in batches if necessary.

5. Add your favorite stir-fry sauce or seasoning for flavor.

6. Stir-fry the broccoli until it is bright green and slightly tender, but still crisp.

7. Combine the tofu and broccoli and stir-fry together briefly to combine flavors.

8. Serve hot over rice or noodles for a complete meal.

Cucumber and cherry tomato salad

Ingredients:

- 2 cucumbers
- 1 pint cherry tomatoes
- 1/4 cup red onion
- 2 tbsp fresh dill
- 2 tbsp olive oil
- 2 tbsp lemon juice
- Salt and pepper to taste

Equipment:

1. Mixing bowl
2. Whisk
3. Knife
4. Cutting board
5. Salad spinner

Methods:

Step 1: Wash and cut 1 cucumber and a cup of cherry tomatoes into bite-sized pieces.

Step 2: In a small bowl, mix 2 tablespoons of olive oil, 1 tablespoon of lemon juice, 1 teaspoon of honey, and salt and pepper to taste.

Step 3: Toss the cucumber and cherry tomatoes in the dressing until well coated.

Step 4: Let the salad sit for 10-15 minutes to marinate and develop flavor.

Step 5: Serve the cucumber and cherry tomato salad as a refreshing side dish or a light and healthy snack. Enjoy!

Helpful Tips:

1. Use English cucumbers for a more crisp and less watery salad.

2. Slice the cucumbers thinly to maximize surface area for the dressing to cling to.

3. Cut the cherry tomatoes in half to release their juices and flavors.

4. Add a sprinkle of salt to the cucumbers and tomatoes to draw out excess water.

5. Use a dressing of olive oil, red wine vinegar, honey, salt, and pepper for a fresh and tangy flavor.

6. Let the salad marinate in the dressing for at least 30 minutes before serving to allow the flavors to meld.

Baked falafel with lemon tahini dressing

Ingredients:
- 1 can chickpeas
- 1 small onion
- 2 cloves garlic
- 1 tsp cumin
- 1/4 cup fresh parsley
- 1 lemon
- 1/4 cup tahini
- 2 tbsp olive oil
- Salt and pepper to taste

Equipment:
1. Baking sheet
2. Mixing bowl
3. Food processor
4. Whisk
5. Serving platter

Methods:
Step 1: Preheat the oven to 375°F.

Step 2: In a food processor, blend chickpeas, onion, garlic, parsley, cumin, coriander, salt, and pepper until well combined.

Step 3: Form mixture into small balls and place on a lined baking sheet.

Step 4: Drizzle falafel balls with olive oil.

Step 5: Bake in preheated oven for 25-30 minutes, flipping halfway through.

Step 6: Meanwhile, prepare the lemon tahini dressing by whisking together tahini, water, lemon juice, garlic powder, and salt in a bowl.

Step 7: Serve baked falafel with lemon tahini dressing drizzled on top. Enjoy!

Helpful Tips:
1. Soak chickpeas overnight to ensure a smooth falafel texture.

2. Blend chickpeas with fresh herbs like cilantro and parsley for added flavor.

3. Add toasted cumin and coriander seeds for a warm, earthy taste.

4. Shape falafel into small patties for even cooking.

5. Bake falafel at a high temperature for a crispy exterior.

6. Whisk tahini with fresh lemon juice and water for a creamy dressing.

7. Drizzle lemon tahini dressing over warm falafel just before serving.

8. Garnish with chopped parsley and a sprinkle of sumac for a pop of color and flavor.

Grilled halibut with tropical fruit salsa

Ingredients:
- 4 halibut fillets
- 1 cup diced mango
- 1/2 cup diced pineapple
- 1/4 cup diced red onion
- 1 tbsp chopped cilantro
- 1 jalapeno, diced
- Salt and pepper to taste

Equipment:
1. Grill pan
2. Tongs
3. Fish spatula
4. Mixing bowl
5. Cutting board
6. Knife

Methods:
Step 1: Preheat the grill to medium-high heat.

Step 2: Season halibut fillets with salt, pepper, and olive oil.

Step 3: Grill the halibut fillets for 4-5 minutes per side, or until cooked through.

Step 4: In a medium bowl, mix diced mango, pineapple, red onion, jalapeno, cilantro, and lime juice to make the tropical fruit salsa.

Step 5: Season the fruit salsa with a pinch of salt and pepper.

Step 6: Serve the grilled halibut topped with the tropical fruit salsa.

Step 7: Enjoy your delicious grilled halibut with tropical fruit salsa!

Helpful Tips:
1. Start by preparing the tropical fruit salsa by combining diced mango, pineapple, red onion, jalapeno, cilantro, lime juice, and salt.

2. Preheat your grill to medium-high heat and lightly oil the grates to prevent sticking.

3. Season the halibut fillets with salt, pepper, and a squeeze of lime juice before grilling.

4. Grill the halibut for about 4-5 minutes per side, or until the fish is opaque and easily flakes with a fork.

5. Top the grilled halibut with the tropical fruit salsa and serve immediately for a fresh and flavorful dish.

6. Pair with a side of quinoa or coconut rice for a complete meal.

Grilled chicken breast with roasted vegetables

Ingredients:

- 4 chicken breasts
- 2 bell peppers
- 1 zucchini
- 1 red onion
- 2 tbsp olive oil
- 1 tsp salt
- 1 tsp pepper

Equipment:

1. Frying pan
2. Baking sheet
3. Tongs
4. Grill pan
5. Knife
6. Cutting board

Methods:

Step 1: Preheat the grill to medium-high heat.

Step 2: Season the chicken breasts with salt, pepper, and your choice of seasoning.

Step 3: Grill the chicken breasts for 6-8 minutes on each side or until cooked through.

Step 4: In a baking dish, toss your favorite vegetables such as bell peppers, zucchini, and cherry tomatoes with olive oil, salt, and pepper.

Step 5: Roast the vegetables in the oven at 400°F for 20-25 minutes or until they are tender.

Step 6: Serve the grilled chicken breasts with the roasted vegetables on the side. Enjoy your delicious and healthy meal!

Helpful Tips:

1. Marinate chicken in a mixture of olive oil, garlic, lemon juice, and your favorite herbs for at least 30 minutes.

2. Preheat your grill to medium-high heat before cooking the chicken.

3. Cook chicken for about 6-7 minutes per side, or until internal temperature reaches 165°F.

4. Toss vegetables (such as bell peppers, zucchini, and cherry tomatoes) in olive oil, salt, and pepper before roasting in the oven at 400°F for 20-25 minutes.

5. Serve the grilled chicken with the roasted vegetables for a healthy and delicious meal. Enjoy!

Baked salmon with lemon and herbs

Ingredients:

- 4 salmon fillets
- 1 lemon, sliced
- 2 tbsp olive oil
- 1 tsp dried thyme
- Salt and pepper to taste

Equipment:

1. Baking sheet
2. Mixing bowl
3. Whisk
4. Knife
5. Cutting board

Methods:

Step 1: Preheat the oven to 400°F and line a baking sheet with parchment paper.

Step 2: Season the salmon fillets with salt and pepper on both sides.

Step 3: Place the salmon on the prepared baking sheet.

Step 4: In a small bowl, mix together melted butter, lemon juice, minced garlic, and chopped fresh herbs (such as dill, parsley, and thyme).

Step 5: Spoon the butter mixture over the salmon fillets.

Step 6: Bake the salmon in the preheated oven for 12-15 minutes, or until it flakes easily with a fork.

Step 7: Serve the baked salmon hot with additional lemon wedges and herbs for garnish. Enjoy!

Helpful Tips:

1. Preheat your oven to 375°F.

2. Season your salmon fillets with salt, pepper, and your favorite herbs (such as dill, parsley, or thyme).

3. Place the seasoned salmon on a baking sheet lined with parchment paper.

4. Squeeze fresh lemon juice over the salmon and top with lemon slices for extra flavor.

5. Drizzle some olive oil over the salmon to keep it moist during baking.

6. Bake the salmon for 12-15 minutes, or until it flakes easily with a fork.

7. Serve the baked salmon with additional lemon wedges and fresh herbs for garnish. Enjoy!

Quinoa salad with fresh vegetables

Ingredients:

- 1 cup quinoa
- 1 cucumber, diced
- 1 bell pepper, diced
- 1 carrot, shredded
- 1/4 cup fresh parsley
- 1/4 cup lemon juice
- 2 tbsp olive oil
- Salt and pepper to taste

Equipment:

1. Knife
2. Cutting board
3. Salad spinner
4. Mixing bowl
5. Tongs

Methods:

Step 1: Rinse 1 cup of quinoa in a fine-mesh strainer under cold water.

Step 2: In a pot, bring 2 cups of water to a boil and add the quinoa. Reduce heat, cover, and let simmer for about 15 minutes.

Step 3: Chop up your favorite fresh vegetables such as tomatoes, cucumbers, bell peppers, and red onions.

Step 4: In a large bowl, combine the cooked quinoa and chopped vegetables.

Step 5: Mix in some fresh herbs like parsley and mint for added flavor.

Step 6: Drizzle with olive oil and lemon juice, and season with salt and pepper to taste.

Step 7: Serve chilled and enjoy your delicious quinoa salad with fresh vegetables.

Helpful Tips:

1. Rinse 1 cup of quinoa thoroughly before cooking to remove any bitter outer coating.

2. Use 2 cups of water or vegetable broth for every cup of quinoa.

3. Bring the water to a boil, then reduce heat to a simmer and cover for 15-20 minutes until all liquid is absorbed.

4. Allow the cooked quinoa to cool before adding in chopped fresh vegetables like bell peppers, cucumbers, tomatoes, and red onions.

5. Dress the salad with a simple vinaigrette made from olive oil, lemon juice, salt, and pepper.

6. Add fresh herbs like parsley or cilantro for extra flavor.

7. Serve chilled or at room temperature for a refreshing side dish or main meal.

Lentil soup with spinach

Ingredients:
- 1 cup of lentils
- 4 cups of vegetable broth
- 2 cups of fresh spinach
- 1 onion, diced

Equipment:
1. Pot
2. Spoon
3. Knife
4. Cutting board
5. Ladle

Methods:
Step 1: Heat olive oil in a large pot over medium heat.

Step 2: Add chopped onions, carrots, and garlic to the pot.

Step 3: Sauté until vegetables are soft, about 5 minutes.

Step 4: Pour in vegetable broth and bring to a boil.

Step 5: Add lentils, diced tomatoes, and spinach to the pot.

Step 6: Season with salt, pepper, and any desired herbs or spices.

Step 7: Simmer for 20-25 minutes, or until lentils are tender.

Step 8: Taste and adjust seasoning as needed.

Step 9: Serve hot with a sprinkle of grated Parmesan cheese on top. Enjoy your delicious Lentil soup with spinach!

Helpful Tips:
1. Start by sautéing onions, garlic, and carrots in a large pot with olive oil.

2. Add vegetable broth, lentils, and diced tomatoes to the pot and bring to a simmer.

3. Season with salt, pepper, and your favorite herbs like cumin or thyme.

4. Let the soup cook for about 30-40 minutes until the lentils are tender.

5. Add fresh spinach to the pot and cook for an additional 5 minutes until wilted.

6. For extra flavor, squeeze some lemon juice into the soup before serving.
7. Garnish with fresh herbs or a dollop of yogurt for a creamy finish.
8. Enjoy your nutritious and filling Lentil Soup with Spinach!

Baked cod with cherry tomatoes

Ingredients:
- 4 cod fillets
- 2 cups cherry tomatoes
- 1/4 cup olive oil
- 2 cloves garlic
- Salt and pepper to taste
(98 characters)

Equipment:
1. Baking sheet
2. Oven-safe dish
3. Knife
4. Cutting board
5. Mixing bowl

Methods:
Step 1: Preheat the oven to 400°F.

Step 2: Season the cod fillets with salt and pepper.

Step 3: Place the cod fillets in a baking dish.

Step 4: Scatter cherry tomatoes around the cod fillets.

Step 5: Drizzle olive oil over the cod and tomatoes.

Step 6: Sprinkle chopped garlic and fresh herbs over the top.

Step 7: Bake in the preheated oven for 15-20 minutes, or until the cod is flaky and cooked through.

Step 8: Serve the baked cod with cherry tomatoes hot, garnished with additional herbs if desired. Enjoy!

Helpful Tips:
1. Preheat your oven to 375°F.
2. Lightly grease a baking dish with olive oil.
3. Season the cod fillets with salt, pepper, and your favorite herbs.
4. Place the seasoned cod fillets in the baking dish.
5. Scatter halved cherry tomatoes over the top of the cod.

6. Drizzle with olive oil and a squeeze of lemon juice.

7. Bake in the preheated oven for 15-20 minutes, or until the fish is opaque and flakes easily with a fork.

8. Serve hot with a side of roasted veggies or a fresh salad.

9. Enjoy your delicious and healthy baked cod with cherry tomatoes!

Chickpea and vegetable curry

Ingredients:
- 2 cans of chickpeas
- 1 eggplant, cubed
- 2 bell peppers, sliced
- 1 onion, chopped
- 2 cloves of garlic, minced
- 1 can of diced tomatoes
- 1 cup of vegetable broth
- 2 tablespoons of curry powder
- Salt and pepper to taste

Equipment:
1. Cutting board
2. Chef's knife
3. Saucepan
4. Wooden spoon
5. Stirring ladle

Methods:
Step 1: Heat oil in a large skillet over medium heat.

Step 2: Add diced onions, minced garlic, and grated ginger to the skillet. Cook until onions are translucent.

Step 3: Stir in curry powder, cumin, turmeric, and coriander. Cook for 1-2 minutes until fragrant.

Step 4: Add diced tomatoes, chickpeas, and vegetable broth. Bring to a simmer and let cook for 15-20 minutes.

Step 5: Stir in diced potatoes, bell peppers, and cauliflower. Cook for an additional 10-15 minutes until vegetables are tender.

Step 6: Serve the chickpea and vegetable curry over rice or with naan bread. Enjoy!

Helpful Tips:
1. Start by sautéing onions, garlic, and ginger in oil until they are fragrant.

2. Add your favorite curry spices such as cumin, turmeric, coriander, and garam masala for a flavorful base.

3. Incorporate chopped tomatoes or tomato paste for a rich, thick sauce.

4. Cook the chickpeas until they are tender and have absorbed the flavors of the curry.

5. Add in your choice of vegetables such as bell peppers, spinach, or carrots for added nutrition.

6. Adjust the seasoning with salt, pepper, or chili flakes to suit your taste.

7. Serve with rice or naan bread for a satisfying meal.

Grilled shrimp skewers with pineapple

Ingredients:
- 1 pound shrimp
- 1/2 pineapple
- 1/4 cup olive oil
- Salt and pepper to taste.

Equipment:
1. Skewers
2. Grill pan
3. Tongs
4. Basting brush
5. Cutting board
6. Knife

Methods:
Step 1: Soak wooden skewers in water for 30 minutes.

Step 2: Preheat grill to medium-high heat.

Step 3: Thread peeled and deveined shrimp onto skewers, alternating with chunks of pineapple.

Step 4: Brush skewers with olive oil and season with salt, pepper, and your favorite seasoning.

Step 5: Grill skewers for 2-3 minutes per side, until shrimp are pink and opaque.

Step 6: Remove skewers from grill and let rest for a few minutes before serving.

Step 7: Optional: Serve with a side of rice and a squeeze of fresh lime juice for added flavor. Enjoy your grilled shrimp skewers with pineapple!

Helpful Tips:
1. Soak wooden skewers in water for at least 30 minutes to prevent burning.

2. Marinate shrimp in a mixture of olive oil, garlic, lemon juice, and herbs for at least 30 minutes.

3. Alternate threading shrimp and pineapple chunks onto skewers for even cooking.

4. Preheat grill to medium-high heat before adding skewers.

5. Grill skewers for 2-3 minutes per side, or until shrimp is pink and opaque.

6. Brush skewers with additional marinade while grilling for extra flavor.

7. Serve skewers hot with a side of rice or mixed greens for a complete meal.

8. Enjoy the sweet and savory combination of grilled shrimp and pineapple!

Turkey meatballs with whole wheat pasta

Ingredients:
- 1 lb ground turkey
- 1/2 cup breadcrumbs
- 1/4 cup grated Parmesan
- 2 cloves garlic, minced
- 1/4 cup chopped parsley
- 1 egg
- Salt and pepper to taste
- 8 oz whole wheat pasta

Equipment:
1. Mixing bowl
2. Whisk
3. Saucepan
4. Skillet
5. Wooden spoon
6. Pasta pot

Methods:
Step 1: Preheat the oven to 375°F.

Step 2: In a large bowl, mix together ground turkey, breadcrumbs, grated Parmesan cheese, minced garlic, chopped parsley, salt, and pepper.

Step 3: Form the mixture into small meatballs and place them on a baking sheet lined with parchment paper.

Step 4: Bake the meatballs in the preheated oven for 20-25 minutes or until fully cooked.

Step 5: In a large pot, cook whole wheat pasta according to package instructions.

Step 6: Once the pasta is cooked, drain and toss with your favorite marinara sauce.

Step 7: Serve the turkey meatballs on top of the whole wheat pasta and garnish with additional Parmesan cheese and parsley. Enjoy!

Helpful Tips:

1. Use lean ground turkey to reduce the fat content in the meatballs.

2. Season the ground turkey well with salt, pepper, garlic powder, and Italian herbs for added flavor.

3. Consider adding finely chopped vegetables like onions, carrots, and bell peppers to the meatball mixture for added nutrients.

4. To bind the meatballs, use whole wheat breadcrumbs instead of white breadcrumbs for a healthier option.

5. Bake the meatballs in the oven instead of frying them to reduce the amount of added oil.

6. Serve the turkey meatballs with whole wheat pasta for a balanced meal rich in protein and fiber.

Brown rice and black bean bowl

Ingredients:
- 2 cups cooked brown rice
- 1 can black beans, drained
- 1 avocado, sliced
- 1/2 cup salsa

Equipment:
1. Pot
2. Pan
3. Knife
4. Cutting board
5. Mixing bowl
6. Spatula

Methods:
Step 1: Rinse 1 cup of brown rice under cold water.

Step 2: In a medium saucepan, combine the rinsed rice with 2 cups of water.

Step 3: Bring the water to a boil, then reduce the heat to low and cover the saucepan with a lid.

Step 4: Cook the rice for 30-40 minutes, or until all the water has been absorbed.

Step 5: In a separate pan, heat 1 tablespoon of olive oil over medium heat.

Step 6: Add 1 can of drained and rinsed black beans to the pan and cook for 5-7 minutes.

Step 7: Serve the cooked rice and beans together in a bowl and enjoy!

Helpful Tips:
1. Rinse the brown rice well before cooking to remove any excess starch.

2. Use a ratio of 2 parts water to 1 part rice for perfectly cooked grains.

3. Cook the rice over low heat for about 40-45 minutes, or until tender.

4. Season the rice with a pinch of salt, pepper, and a drizzle of olive oil for extra flavor.

5. Drain and rinse canned black beans before adding them to the rice bowl.

6. Season the black beans with your favorite spices, such as cumin, garlic powder, and paprika.

7. Garnish the bowl with fresh herbs, avocado slices, and a squeeze of lime juice for a burst of freshness.

Baked halibut with asparagus

Ingredients:
- 4 halibut fillets
- 1 bunch of asparagus
- 4 tbsp olive oil
- Salt and pepper to taste

Equipment:
1. Baking dish
2. Grill pan
3. Tongs
4. Basting brush
5. Aluminum foil
6. Serving platter

Methods:
Step 1: Preheat the oven to 400°F.

Step 2: Place the halibut fillets on a baking dish and season with salt, pepper, and a drizzle of olive oil.

Step 3: Arrange the asparagus around the halibut fillets and drizzle with olive oil, salt, and pepper.

Step 4: Place the baking dish in the oven and bake for 15-20 minutes, or until the fish is cooked through and the asparagus is tender.

Step 5: Remove from the oven and serve hot, garnished with lemon wedges and fresh herbs. Enjoy your delicious baked halibut with asparagus meal!

Helpful Tips:
1. Preheat your oven to 400°F and season the halibut with salt, pepper, and your choice of herbs.

2. Place the seasoned halibut on a baking sheet lined with parchment paper.

3. Drizzle olive oil over the halibut and bake for 12-15 minutes or until the fish is cooked through.

4. While the halibut is baking, toss asparagus spears with olive oil, salt, and pepper.

5. Arrange the asparagus on a separate baking sheet and roast in the oven for 10-12 minutes.

6. Serve the baked halibut with the roasted asparagus for a delicious and healthy meal.

Hummus and vegetable wrap

Ingredients:

- 1 cup hummus
- 4 whole wheat wraps
- 2 cups mixed vegetables
- 1/2 cup feta cheese

Equipment:

1. Knife
2. Cutting board
3. Mixing bowl
4. Saute pan
5. Spatula

Methods:

Step 1: Start by rinsing and draining a can of chickpeas.

Step 2: Combine the chickpeas, garlic, lemon juice, tahini, cumin, and olive oil in a food processor.

Step 3: Blend the mixture until smooth, adding water as needed to reach your desired consistency.

Step 4: Season with salt and pepper to taste.

Step 5: Spread the hummus onto a tortilla wrap.

Step 6: Top with sliced cucumbers, tomatoes, red onion, and bell peppers.

Step 7: Roll up the wrap tightly and slice in half.

Step 8: Enjoy your delicious and nutritious hummus and vegetable wrap!

Helpful Tips:

1. Start by preparing your hummus from scratch or using store-bought hummus as a time-saving option.

2. Choose a variety of fresh vegetables for your wrap, such as cucumber, bell peppers, carrots, and avocado.

3. Wash and chop your vegetables into bite-sized pieces for easy assembly.

4. Warm your tortilla or flatbread in a skillet or microwave for a few seconds to make it easier to roll.

5. Spread a generous amount of hummus onto the tortilla, leaving space around the edges for folding.

6. Layer the chopped vegetables on top of the hummus in a colorful arrangement.

7. Roll up the wrap tightly, tucking in the sides as you go to prevent filling from falling out.

8. Secure with toothpicks or wrap in parchment paper for easy transportation.

9. Serve as a healthy and satisfying lunch or snack option. Enjoy!

Baked sweet potato with black beans

Ingredients:

- 4 sweet potatoes
- 1 can black beans
- 1/2 cup shredded cheese
- 1/4 cup chopped cilantro

Equipment:

1. Baking sheet
2. Knife
3. Cutting board
4. Oven
5. Mixing bowl

Methods:

Step 1: Preheat the oven to 400°F.

Step 2: Scrub two sweet potatoes and pierce them several times with a fork.

Step 3: Place the sweet potatoes on a baking sheet and bake for 45-60 minutes, or until tender.

Step 4: In a saucepan, heat a can of black beans with spices of your choice.

Step 5: Once the sweet potatoes are cooked, split them open and fluff the insides with a fork.

Step 6: Top each sweet potato with the black beans mixture.

Step 7: Garnish with chopped fresh cilantro, avocado, and a dollop of Greek yogurt.

Step 8: Enjoy your baked sweet potato with black beans!

Helpful Tips:

1. Preheat your oven to 400°F before you start.

2. Scrub the sweet potatoes thoroughly and pat them dry with a paper towel.

3. Pierce each sweet potato a few times with a fork to allow steam to escape while baking.

4. Rub the sweet potatoes with olive oil and season with salt and pepper before placing them on a baking sheet.

5. Bake for 45-60 minutes or until the sweet potatoes are tender when pierced with a fork.

6. While the sweet potatoes are baking, rinse and drain a can of black beans.

7. Mix the black beans with your favorite seasonings like cumin, garlic powder, and chili powder.

8. When the sweet potatoes are done, slice them open and top with the seasoned black beans.

9. Garnish with fresh cilantro, avocado, and a squeeze of lime juice before serving. Enjoy!

Lemon garlic shrimp with quinoa

Ingredients:
- 1 lb shrimp
- 1 lemon
- 4 cloves garlic
- 1 cup quinoa
- 1 tbsp olive oil
- Salt and pepper to taste

Equipment:
1. Skillet
2. Wooden spoon
3. Tongs
4. Knife
5. Cutting board

Methods:
Step 1: In a large skillet, heat olive oil over medium heat.

Step 2: Add minced garlic and sauté until fragrant, about 1 minute.

Step 3: Add peeled and deveined shrimp to the skillet and cook until pink and cooked through, about 2-3 minutes per side.

Step 4: Squeeze fresh lemon juice over the shrimp and stir to combine.

Step 5: Season with salt and pepper to taste.

Step 6: In a separate saucepan, cook quinoa according to package instructions.

Step 7: Serve the lemon garlic shrimp over the cooked quinoa.

Step 8: Garnish with fresh parsley and enjoy!

Helpful Tips:
1. Start by cooking the quinoa in a separate pot according to package instructions.

2. Marinate the shrimp in a mixture of lemon juice, minced garlic, olive oil, salt, and pepper for at least 20 minutes.

3. Heat a large skillet over medium-high heat and add the marinated shrimp, cooking for 2-3 minutes on each side until pink and opaque.

4. Remove the shrimp from the skillet and set aside.

5. In the same skillet, add a bit more olive oil and sauté some chopped garlic until fragrant.

6. Add cooked quinoa to the skillet and toss to combine with the garlic.

7. Serve the lemon garlic shrimp on top of the garlic quinoa for a delicious and healthy meal.

Vegetable and bean soup

Ingredients:

- 1 onion (diced)
- 2 carrots (sliced)
- 2 stalks of celery (chopped)
- 1 can of diced tomatoes
- 1 can of kidney beans
- 4 cups of vegetable broth
- 1 tsp of cumin
- Salt and pepper to taste

Equipment:

1. Wooden spoon
2. Ladle
3. Chef's knife
4. Cutting board
5. Pot
6. Blender

Methods:

Step 1: Heat olive oil in a large pot over medium heat.

Step 2: Add chopped onions, carrots, and celery to the pot and cook until soft.

Step 3: Stir in minced garlic and cook for another minute.

Step 4: Add diced tomatoes, vegetable broth, and a can of rinsed beans to the pot.

Step 5: Season with salt, pepper, and dried herbs like thyme and oregano.

Step 6: Bring the soup to a boil, then reduce heat and let it simmer for about 20 minutes.

Step 7: Add chopped spinach or kale to the soup and cook until wilted.

Step 8: Serve hot and enjoy!

Helpful Tips:

1. Start by sautéing onions and garlic in olive oil for added flavor.

2. Use a mix of fresh and canned beans for variety and convenience.

3. Don't be afraid to experiment with different vegetables like carrots, celery, and bell peppers.

4. Add vegetable broth or water for a base, and season with herbs and spices like thyme, oregano, and bay leaves.

5. Let the soup simmer for at least 30 minutes to allow the flavors to meld together.

6. Consider blending a portion of the soup for a thicker consistency, or leaving it chunky for added texture.

7. Serve with a side of crusty bread or a sprinkle of Parmesan cheese for a delicious meal.

Egg white omelette with spinach and tomatoes

Ingredients:

- 8 egg whites
- 1 cup chopped spinach
- 1 cup diced tomatoes
- Salt and pepper to taste

Equipment:

1. Frying pan
2. Whisk
3. Spatula
4. Cutting board
5. Knife

Methods:

Step 1: Heat a nonstick skillet over medium heat.

Step 2: Whisk together egg whites in a bowl until frothy.

Step 3: Add spinach and tomatoes to the skillet and sauté until wilted.

Step 4: Pour egg whites into the skillet, swirling to cover the bottom.

Step 5: Cook until the edges start to set, about 2 minutes.

Step 6: Use a spatula to gently lift the edges and let uncooked egg flow underneath.

Step 7: Once the omelette is mostly set, fold it in half.

Step 8: Cook for another minute, then slide onto a plate and serve hot.

Helpful Tips:

1. Start by whisking the egg whites until they are foamy and slightly stiff.

2. Heat a non-stick skillet over medium heat and add in a bit of oil or butter.

3. Pour in the whisked egg whites and let them set for a minute or so.

4. Add in the spinach and tomatoes, season with salt and pepper, and gently fold the omelette in half.

5. Cook for another minute or two until the veggies are heated through.

6. Serve hot and garnish with fresh herbs or a sprinkle of cheese if desired.

7. Enjoy a healthy and delicious breakfast or light meal!

Baked chicken tenders with whole wheat breadcrumbs

Ingredients:
- 1 lb chicken tenders
- 1 cup whole wheat breadcrumbs
- 2 tbsp olive oil
- 1 tsp salt
- 1/2 tsp pepper
- Fresh herbs, optional

Equipment:
1. Baking sheet
2. Tongs
3. Mixing bowl
4. Wire rack
5. Knife
6. Cutting board

Methods:

Step 1: Preheat the oven to 400°F and line a baking sheet with parchment paper.

Step 2: In a shallow dish, mix together whole wheat breadcrumbs, grated Parmesan cheese, garlic powder, salt, and pepper.

Step 3: Dredge each chicken tender in whole wheat flour, then dip into beaten eggs, and finally coat in the breadcrumb mixture.

Step 4: Place the coated chicken tenders onto the prepared baking sheet.

Step 5: Drizzle olive oil over the chicken tenders and bake for 20-25 minutes, or until golden brown and cooked through.

Step 6: Serve hot and enjoy your delicious baked chicken tenders.

Helpful Tips:

1. Preheat your oven to 400°F before you start preparing the chicken tenders.

2. Coat the chicken tenders in a thin layer of olive oil to help the breadcrumbs stick.

3. Use whole wheat breadcrumbs for a healthier alternative to traditional breadcrumbs.

4. Season the breadcrumbs with herbs and spices like garlic powder, paprika, and black pepper for added flavor.

5. Place the chicken tenders on a baking sheet lined with parchment paper to prevent sticking.

6. Bake the chicken tenders for 20-25 minutes or until they are golden brown and cooked through.

7. Serve with your favorite dipping sauce or a side of vegetables for a complete meal.

Spinach and mushroom quiche

Ingredients:
- 1 pre-made pie crust
- 2 cups fresh spinach
- 1 cup sliced mushrooms
- 4 eggs, beaten
- 1 cup shredded cheese
- 1 cup milk
- Salt and pepper to taste

Equipment:
1. Mixing bowl
2. Whisk
3. Pie dish
4. Skillet
5. Knife

Methods:
Step 1: Preheat your oven to 375°F.

Step 2: In a skillet, sauté 1 cup of sliced mushrooms and 2 cups of chopped spinach until wilted.

Step 3: In a bowl, whisk together 4 eggs, 1 cup of milk, and salt and pepper to taste.

Step 4: Roll out a pre-made pie crust and place it in a pie dish.

Step 5: Sprinkle the mushroom and spinach mixture over the crust.

Step 6: Pour the egg mixture over the vegetables.

Step 7: Bake the quiche in the preheated oven for 35-40 minutes, or until the center is set.

Step 8: Let it cool before slicing and serving. Enjoy your spinach and mushroom quiche!

Helpful Tips:
1. Start by preheating your oven to 375°F and lightly grease a pie dish.

2. Roll out your pie crust and press it into the prepared dish, trimming any excess dough.

3. In a skillet, sauté diced onions and garlic until soft, then add sliced mushrooms and spinach. Cook until spinach is wilted.

4. In a mixing bowl, whisk together eggs, milk, salt, pepper, and grated cheese.

5. Add the sautéed vegetables to the egg mixture and pour it into the pie crust.

6. Bake for 35-40 minutes, or until the quiche is set and lightly golden brown.

7. Allow to cool slightly before slicing and serving. Enjoy your delicious spinach and mushroom quiche!

Baked tilapia with mango salsa

Ingredients:
- 4 tilapia fillets
- 1 mango, diced
- 1/4 cup red onion, chopped
- 1/4 cup cilantro, chopped
- 1 jalapeno, diced
- Juice of 1 lime
- 1 tsp olive oil
- Salt and pepper to taste

Equipment:
1. Baking dish
2. Mixing bowl
3. Measuring cups and spoons
4. Baking sheet
5. Knife
6. Cutting board

Methods:
Step 1: Preheat the oven to 400°F and line a baking sheet with parchment paper.

Step 2: Place tilapia fillets on the prepared baking sheet and drizzle with olive oil.

Step 3: Season the fillets with salt, pepper, and a sprinkle of paprika.

Step 4: Bake the tilapia in the preheated oven for 15-20 minutes, or until cooked through and flakes easily with a fork.

Step 5: While the tilapia is baking, prepare the mango salsa by combining diced mango, red onion, jalapeno, cilantro, lime juice, and salt in a bowl.

Step 6: Serve the baked tilapia topped with the mango salsa and enjoy!

Helpful Tips:
1. Start by marinating the tilapia in a mixture of lemon juice, olive oil, and your choice of seasonings for at least 20 minutes.

2. Preheat the oven to 400°F and line a baking sheet with parchment paper.

3. Place the marinated tilapia on the baking sheet and cook for 10-12 minutes until the fish is flaky and opaque.

4. While the tilapia is cooking, prepare the mango salsa by combining diced mango, red onion, cilantro, lime juice, and jalapeno in a bowl.

5. Season the salsa with salt and pepper to taste and let it sit for flavors to meld.

6. Serve the baked tilapia topped with the mango salsa for a fresh and flavorful meal.

Cucumber and tomato salad

Ingredients:

- 2 cucumbers
- 4 tomatoes
- 1/4 cup red onion
- 1/4 cup feta cheese
- 2 tbsp olive oil
- 1 tbsp red wine vinegar
- Salt and pepper, to taste

Equipment:

1. Knife
2. Cutting board
3. Mixing bowl
4. Salad tongs
5. Serving bowl

Methods:

Step 1: Wash and dry the cucumber and tomato.

Step 2: Cut the cucumber and tomato into bite-sized pieces.

Step 3: In a mixing bowl, combine the cucumber and tomato pieces.

Step 4: Add some finely chopped red onion and fresh herbs, such as parsley or mint.

Step 5: Drizzle some olive oil and lemon juice over the salad.

Step 6: Season with salt and pepper to taste.

Step 7: Toss everything together until well combined.

Step 8: Let the salad sit for a few minutes to allow the flavors to meld together.

Step 9: Serve the cucumber and tomato salad chilled and enjoy!

Helpful Tips:

1. Use fresh, ripe cucumbers and tomatoes for the best flavor.

2. Wash and chop the vegetables into uniform pieces for a visually appealing salad.

3. Add a sprinkle of salt to the cucumbers to draw out excess moisture.

4. Consider adding thinly sliced red onion or fresh herbs like parsley or dill for extra flavor.

5. Dress the salad with a simple vinaigrette of olive oil, vinegar, salt, and pepper.

6. Allow the salad to sit in the fridge for at least 30 minutes before serving to let the flavors meld.

7. Serve the cucumber and tomato salad as a refreshing side dish or topping for grilled meats.

Roasted cauliflower with Parmesan cheese

Ingredients:
- 1 head cauliflower
- 2 tbsp olive oil
- 1/4 cup grated Parmesan cheese
- Salt and pepper to taste

Equipment:
1. Baking sheet
2. Mixing bowl
3. Knife
4. Grater
5. Oven
6. Serving plate

Methods:
Step 1: Preheat the oven to 400°F (200°C).

Step 2: Cut a head of cauliflower into florets and spread them out on a baking sheet.

Step 3: Drizzle olive oil over the cauliflower and season with salt and pepper.

Step 4: Roast the cauliflower in the oven for 25-30 minutes, or until golden brown and tender.

Step 5: Sprinkle grated Parmesan cheese over the cauliflower and return to the oven for another 5 minutes, until the cheese is melted and bubbly.

Step 6: Remove from the oven and garnish with chopped parsley or red pepper flakes, if desired.

Step 7: Serve hot and enjoy your delicious roasted cauliflower with Parmesan cheese!

Helpful Tips:
1. Preheat the oven to 400°F.
2. Cut the cauliflower into florets and place them in a large bowl.
3. Drizzle with olive oil and toss to coat evenly.

4. Season with salt, pepper, and any desired herbs or spices.

5. Spread the cauliflower out on a baking sheet in a single layer.

6. Roast in the oven for 25-30 minutes, or until the cauliflower is golden brown and tender.

7. Sprinkle with freshly grated Parmesan cheese before serving.

8. Garnish with chopped parsley or lemon zest for extra flavor.

9. Serve hot as a delicious side dish or snack. Enjoy!

9 798223 702726